RAY MEARS

THE REAL HEROES
OF TELEMARK

D0094478

CORONET BOOKS
Hodder & Stoughton

Copyright © 2003 by Ray Mears

First published in Great Britain in 2003 by Hodder & Stoughton
A division of Hodder Headline

This edition published in 2004

By arrangement with the BBC
The BBC logo is a registered trademark of the British Broadcasting
Corporation and is used under licence.
BBC logo © BBC 1996.

A CIP catalogue record for this title is available from the British Library

ISBN 978-0-340-83016-1

Map by Neil Gower

Typeset in 12/17 Monotype Sabon by Servis Filmsetting Ltd, Manchester
Printed and bound in Great Britain by Clays Ltd, St Ives plc

Hodder and Stoughton
A division of Hodder Headline
338 Euston Road
London NW1 3BH

THE REAL HEROES
OF TELEMARK

A man who is a man goes on till he can do no more and then goes twice as far.

Norwegian saying

In the skies above London
In the African desert
In the ruins of Stalingrad
And on the Normandy beaches
Norway was given back to us.

Tribute in Norwegian Resistance Museum in Oslo

You opened your homes
And your hearts to us
And gave us hope.

Norwegian tribute on memorial at Glenmore

CONTENTS

LIST OF MAIN CHARACTERS

OPERATION GROUSE (LATER CALLED SWALLOW)

Second Lieutenant Jens Anton Poulsson (leader)
Second Lieutenant Knut Haugland (W/T operator)
Sergeant Claus Helberg
Sergeant Arne Kjelstrup

OPERATION GUNNERSIDE

Second Lieutenant Joachim Rønneberg (leader)
Second Lieutenant Knut Haukelid (originally member of Grouse)
Second Lieutenant Kasper Idland
Sergeant Fredrik Kayser
Sergeant Hans Storhaug
Sergeant Birger Strømsheim

OTHERS

Einar Skinnarland (Special Operations Executive agent, Grouse
    contact at Vemork plant)
Professor Leif Tronstad (former manager of Vemork, leading
    scientist, Norwegian Army officer seconded to SOE, operations
    planner)
Major-General Sir Colin Gubbins (chief of SOE)
Lieutenant Colonel Jack Wilson (head of SOE training, SOE
    Norwegian section)
Reichskommissar Josef Terboven (leading German official in Norway)
General Nikolaus von Falkenhorst (commander-in-chief of German
    forces in Norway)

FOREWORD

While filming in Scotland a few years ago, I came across what remains of a military training camp at Drumintoul near Aviemore. Locals told me about the thousands of young Norwegians who had passed through the centre during the Second World War as recruits of the Special Operations Executive (SOE), the forerunners of the SAS. One story in particular fired my curiosity: a raid by a group of these men on a hydroelectric plant in the frozen wilderness of Norway's Telemark region.

As an outdoorsman and a teacher of survival skills, I was especially enthralled by the accounts of these men using their native knowledge to live on the Hardangervidda, Europe's largest high plateau. As a passionate student of nature, I wanted to know more about this great wilderness sitting on our very doorstep. As a lover of adventure, my imagination was also seized by the details of the military operations that make up the story. They sounded like something straight out of those commando magazines we used to read as young boys. But this story is true! As a human being, I was awestruck by the spirit and courage the men must have possessed – or discovered within themselves – just to survive, let alone attempt one of the most audacious sabotage acts in the history of warfare.

When you consider the story in its wider historical context and understand the stakes involved for those fighting on the side of peace and freedom during that bloodiest of conflicts, its power and drama become almost overwhelming.

I wanted to find out more, and so during a break in my filming schedule I flew to Oslo and visited the Norwegian Resistance Museum tucked away inside the city's ancient Akershus Castle. At this stage I had no thoughts about making a television series or writing a book. I was just curious and wanted to find out more. I had seen the 1965 Hollywood film *The Heroes of Telemark* and could remember the odd scene from it, but I soon learned that this representation of the events was a dreadful travesty of the truth. (In fact, the truth is far more captivating that the bastardised version of it that found its way on to the silver screen.)

From Oslo I headed up to the Telemark region and saw for myself the now defunct hydroelectric plant at Vemork which forms the focus of the story. It is a forbidding place whichever way you look at it, and regardless of the friendliness of the people who live along the floor of the dark narrow valley in which it is situated. I travelled a few kilometres up the valley's winding road and saw the beautiful bleakness of the Hardangervidda stretching out over the horizon, and it was then that I understood the real triumph of the men of Operation Grouse and Operation Gunnerside.

Ray Mears, June 2003

PROLOGUE

On 17 June 1942, a Boeing flying boat carrying Winston Churchill thundered into the early evening sky from Stranraer on the south-west coast of Scotland on its way to the United States. The Prime Minister was heading to New York for a meeting with President Franklin Roosevelt, and he had plenty to exercise his mind as he sipped his first drink of the flight and watched the sun begin to set over the Atlantic at the start of a twenty-six hour journey. In the vast expanse of ocean below, the drama of the war was being played out as hundreds of ships carrying vital supplies for the British people and the Allied war effort headed nervously in the opposite direction. Below the surface, hundreds of German U-boats laden with torpedoes were busy hunting down the ships, poised to wreak more havoc on a nation already brought close to breaking point after three years of struggle against the most powerful war machine ever sent into battle under the command of one of the most brutal dictators in history.

Britain no longer stood alone, but time was ebbing away on all fronts as America primed its people and its industry for a long, painful struggle to liberate the world from the tyranny of Nazi occupation in the West and Japanese imperialism in the East.

Britain had yet to win a significant battle on the ground, half its capital city lay in smouldering rubble, Rommel's Afrika Korps had seized the initiative in North Africa, the so-called fortress of Singapore had surrendered to the Japanese, America was still punch-drunk from the attack on Pearl Harbor the previous year, and Western Europe was no longer a battlefield but an annexe of Nazi Germany.

But of all the fears and anxieties swirling around Churchill's mind, one in particular kept pushing itself to the forefront of his thoughts. It was water. 'Heavy' water. As far as he understood it from his scientific adviser, Lord Cherwell, Churchill could, if he so wished, take the water with his whisky, he could bathe in it or water his flowers with it at Chartwell, his country home in Kent. He could even feed it to his young grandchildren. It looked and tasted utterly harmless. Only if it was frozen into cubes and dropped into an ordinary glass of water would he have realised that there was something very peculiar about this substance. The cubes would sink to the bottom of the glass.

There were only a few hundred pounds of heavy water on the planet at this time, but it was worth more than the world's entire gold reserves to the small handful of people who understood its terrible potential. Heavy water was a prerequisite for building the world's first 'atomic bomb' – an expression that would have meant absolutely nothing at the time to an ordinary member of the public. Atomic power, no more than a discussion topic for physicists a few years earlier, was rapidly becoming an awful reality, and only a handful of scientists, military chiefs and high-ranking politicians on either side of the conflict understood the dangers.

Most of the world's heavy water was sitting in a dozen or so canisters in a heavily fortified hydroelectric plant deep in the wilderness of occupied Norway. Drip by drip its volume was growing, and with every tiny splash Hitler edged closer to visiting devastation on the civilised world. London was the Führer's prime target. If he could knock out the centre of the British capital at a stroke, the war would be won. Britain would be forced to surrender under threat of a second strike, and the United States would no longer have the springboard needed to launch the campaign to free mainland Europe.

Never in the entire conflict did Hitler have greater reason to feel convinced that he stood on the brink of conquering the Western world. Most of Europe lay helplessly in the iron grip of the Nazis or their allies. France, Poland, Denmark, Austria, Norway, Italy, Greece, Belgium, the Netherlands, Czechoslovakia, Hungary, Romania and Yugoslavia had all succumbed. By the winter of 1941 German troops had advanced across the rolling plains of the Soviet Union to within just a few miles of Moscow. North Africa, too, was the scene of a violent tug-of-war between British and Commonwealth troops on the one side and Germans and Italians on the other. The neutral countries of Sweden, Spain and Switzerland all kept their heads down, fearful of provoking the Axis powers into an invasion.

Only the United Kingdom remained truly free, but the people's morale and resources were being stretched to the limit by a series of setbacks on the battlefields, the pounding of her cities by the Luftwaffe and the U-boat campaign in the Atlantic, which was destroying tens of thousands of vital supplies by the week. The Battle of Britain in the summer of 1940, however, had at least thwarted Hitler's invasion plans and provided a beacon of hope for occupied Europe.

While the Wehrmacht were crushing all that stood in the way of their blitzkrieg sweep through Europe and North Africa, Hitler's scientists were comfortably winning the race behind the scenes to develop a weapon of destruction so mighty that the mere threat of its use would be sufficient to secure Nazi hegemony wherever in the world he chose to have it. Churchill had initially been sceptical about Germany's ability to invent a bomb capable of reducing an entire city to rubble and radioactive dust. In August 1939, just before the outbreak of war, he had written that the fear of 'some sinister, new secret explosive with which to destroy their enemies is clearly without foundation'. Only a few leading scientists understood the new threat. Albert Einstein had written to President Roosevelt warning him of the rapid strides being made in the study of atomic energy.

It may be possible to set up a nuclear chain reaction in a large mass of uranium, by which vast amounts of power and large quantities of new radium-like elements would be generated. Now it appears almost certain that this could be achieved in the immediate future.

This new phenomenon would also lead to the construction of bombs, and it is conceivable, though much less certain, that extremely powerful bombs of a new type may thus be constructed. A single bomb of this type, carried by boat and exploded in a port, might well destroy the whole port together with some of the surrounding territory.

As Churchill's flying boat rumbled its away across the Atlantic, a group of young Norwegians were preparing to retire to their beds back in Britain. Like Churchill, they too were tired, worried and itching for a proper fight with the forces that had brought so much misery to their world. They were tired because they had just come to the end of another gruelling day training under the auspices of the Special Operations Executive (SOE), the world's first secret army established shortly after the outbreak of war with the aim of disrupting Germany from within, through sabotage and guerrilla warfare. (Or, as Churchill put it later, 'to set Europe ablaze'.) They were worried because they had had no news of their friends and families back in Norway and they could see no immediate prospect of the invaders being expelled and their homeland liberated. They were itching for a fight because they were fanatical patriots who had risked their lives to escape to Britain and join the Allied war effort.

Across the other side of the planet, the sun was starting to rise on the Japanese Empire. The people of Hiroshima and Nagasaki, like those of other Japanese cities and towns, were busy preparing for another day in a glorious era of their history. The might of the Imperial army, navy and air force had smashed all resistance as they swept through the Far East. But the clock was ticking for them too.

1

The Stakes

On the night of 9 April 1940, Germany launched a lightning attack on Norway. Within twenty-four hours they had seized control of every major city, town, airfield and military installation. It was a shocking night for the sleepy Scandinavian country, ushering in five years of occupation, death, deprivation and despair.

Only 12,000 troops spearheaded the invasion but they were supported by 1,200 planes and virtually the full might of the German Navy. The Norwegians' tiny, lightly armed troops were no match for the German war machine with its screeching dive-bombers and heavy tanks, while their Fokker biplanes were useless against the high-tech firepower of the Luftwaffe. A day after the blitzkrieg was launched, Germany's top military brass were checking into Oslo's main hotel next door to Norway's parliament as troops seized control of the country's main towns along the coast: Stavanger, Bergen, Trondheim, Kristiansand and Narvik. Paratroopers seized the Fornebu and Sola airfields and the Swastika was run up the flagpole at Akershus Castle, the headquarters of the Norwegian military and a symbol of national pride.

After 125 years of peace, living on the outer fringes of international affairs, Norway was totally unprepared for the lightning assault and the Germans had little problem in overrunning the rest of the country in the coming weeks. Within just a few days Wehrmacht soldiers were able to walk into towns and villages without resistance and nail propaganda and information notices to billboards and telegraph poles. There was some sporadic resistance, but it was difficult for the Norwegians to form themselves into effective units and defensive formations after they had been caught sleeping, literally and figuratively, on the night of the invasion. The greatest damage the Norwegians were able to inflict on the invaders came on the first night of the attack when two ancient guns in Oscarsborg Fort sank the heavy cruiser *Blücher* with 1,000 hands on board. Crucially, the sinking of one of the flagships of the German Navy allowed King Haakon VII and his government to escape – by a matter of hours – to the north, from where they fled to London on the *HMS Devonshire* on 7 June to join seven other governments-in-exile. It took just sixty days for Hitler to annex the country.

Norway was of the highest strategic importance to Hitler as it provided him with a long coastline and deep fjords from where his ships and U-boats could attack Allied convoys crossing the Atlantic and Royal Navy ships attempting their own blockade of Germany. But its collapse brought with it a threat of an entirely different order of magnitude. In a remote valley in the Telemark region, about 150 miles west of Oslo, lay the Norsk Hydro Plant at Vemork, just outside the town of Rjukan. Its production was every bit as forbidding and awesome as its appearance and setting. Situated halfway up an almost sheer cliff face in a narrow sunless valley, the giant rumbling machinery of the plant, over the previous decade, had slowly been producing the world's only significant stocks of heavy water, a by-product of the hydrogen being generated for the development of fertilisers.

Nuclear physics was still very much in its infancy when in 1938 the German scientists Otto Hahn and Fritz Strassman successfully split the uranium nucleus, releasing atomic energy for the first time. The next step was to create a chain reaction, and this is where heavy water came in. Deuterium oxide, to give it its scientific name, is an excellent 'braking' medium, causing chemical and biological processes to happen at a far slower rate than in ordinary water. By slowing down neutrons as they pass through the heavy water, scientists had found a way of developing a controlled fission process in uranium. Energy could then be harnessed for the creation of an explosion a hundred times greater than in any conventional bomb.

In the 1930s physicists around the world were largely happy to share their findings about the development of atomic power. But once the threat of hostilities began, a frantic race between the Allies and the Axis powers was set in motion. It is no exaggeration to say that upon this race rested the destiny of the Second World War and, by extension, the very future of Western civilisation.

A tiny quantity of heavy water is found in ordinary water, but the task of separating it was then extremely slow and laborious. This gave the Allies a little breathing space as they set about making plans to undermine German research and development in this field. Experts at the time disagreed over the exact timescale involved in producing an atomic bomb, but there was general consensus that one side would get there within two to five years. In the United States, the atomic bomb programme was known as the 'Manhattan Project', and considerable funds were made available to it by the government to try to enable scientists to catch up with the Germans in this field.

To the relief of the Allies, the entire stock of Vemork's heavy water had been smuggled out of Norway shortly before the invasion by the eminent French scientist Frederic Joliot-Curie under the very noses of German agents. Placing twenty-six dummy canisters on a plane to Amsterdam as the Germans looked on, Joliot-Curie himself boarded the plane, then promptly stepped out the other side and boarded another containing the real stocks before taking off for Scotland. The priceless cargo was then taken to Paris, but it was hastily transported south when the Germans invaded France and advanced towards the capital. From there, the canisters were eventually removed to the safety of Britain.

This was a significant blow for the Germans, but they had another problem too. Many of the country's top scientists were Jews who had fled the country to escape persecution, taking their knowledge over to the Allies. But despite the setbacks they remained streets ahead of the Allies in their development programme at the start of the war.

In May 1941 alarm spread through the corridors of Whitehall when intelligence sources reported that the Germans had ordered a tenfold increase in production of heavy water at Vemork, to 3,000 pounds per year. Unease turned to near-panic by the end of the year when the news arrived that the Germans had ordered that production be increased threefold to 10,000 pounds per year, triggering a blizzard of 'Most Secret' memoranda between Downing Street, the War Office and other departments in Whitehall. There could now be no doubt that Hitler was exerting the greatest pressure on his scientists to beat the Allies in the race to build an atomic weapon. (When contact was secretly made with the managers at Vemork, British intelligence received a message saying that the Norwegians were prepared to cooperate but only after they received an assurance that the rival British firm ICI was not behind the request to damage or destroy the heavy water stocks. Blood, the Norwegians said, was 'thicker even than heavy water'.)

The original development of heavy water at Vemork had been overseen by Professor Leif Tronstad, a fervent patriot and a brilliant scientist. No one knew the plant's layout or the details of the production process better than him. The Germans ordered Tronstad to supervise the rapid construction of the apparatus needed to produce the heavy water at the dramatically increased rates. Tronstad tried to slow the process down as much as possible, without jeopardising his own position, by delaying the construction of new apparatus and injecting small quantities of castor oil and cod liver oil into existing stocks. In the summer of 1941 the professor was warned that the Germans were growing suspicious of him, and he soon received orders from London to leave as quickly as possible.

After bidding a painful farewell to his family he fled to neutral Sweden before heading to Britain. Shortly after his arrival he was appointed head of Section IV of the Norwegian High Command, with responsibility for coordinating intelligence and sabotage activities in Norway in conjunction with SOE, Britain's highly secret army specialising in 'irregular' warfare. Dr Jomar Brun, who had collaborated with Tronstad in the development of the heavy water, became the plant's new chief manager. He was also a 'Jøssing' (a true Norwegian), and became a vital source of intelligence for the Allies, sending messages via SOE or by microphotographs concealed in toothpaste tubes which were smuggled across the frontier to Sweden and then on to the UK.

It was not long into his premiership before Churchill revised his opinions about Germany's atomic threat as the scientific evidence began to mount on both sides of the conflict that such power could be ready for use in the very near future. His scientific adviser, Lord Cherwell, had prepared a report on nuclear research, prior to the Prime Minister's visit to the United States in that summer of 1942, in which he wrote: 'It would be unforgivable if we let the Germans develop a process ahead of us by means of which they could defeat us or reverse the verdict after they had been defeated.'

By the time Churchill and Roosevelt met in New York neither needed any more siren warnings from the scientific community to convince them of the threat that faced their people. The two leaders of the free world agreed that no resource or effort should be spared both in the pursuit of creating a new 'super-explosive' and in the effort to undermine Germany's own progress. 'We both felt painfully the dangers of doing nothing,' Churchill wrote later of his meeting with the American President.

Once news of the activities at Vemork had passed from scientific and intelligence circles into military and political spheres, it was only logical that officials in Whitehall should make contact with the chiefs of SOE. The need for covert operations involving intelligence-gathering and sabotage acts against German military and economic interests deep behind enemy lines was the very reason it had been brought into existence. Dr Hugh Dalton, the Minister of Economic Warfare, was one of the architects of SOE's formation and had gone to great lengths to persuade his Cabinet colleagues that such an organisation would have a significant impact on the German regime.

Churchill had his suspicions about Dalton, a Labour member

of the coalition government, as well as about the merits of guerrilla warfare, but he admired the man's aggression and energy
and was prepared to consider any means of hurting the Germans
before a full-scale invasion of Europe became a realistic prospect. Dalton presented a vivid vision of a new guerrilla warfare
organisation to the Foreign Secretary, Lord Halifax.

> We have got to organize movements in enemy-occupied ter-
> ritory comparable to the Sinn Fein movement in Ireland, to
> the Chinese Guerrillas now operating against Japan, to the
> Spanish Irregulars who played such a notable part in
> Wellington's campaign. Or one might as well admit to the
> organization that the Nazis themselves have developed so
> remarkably well, in almost every country that they are
> involved with.
>
> We must use many different methods, including indus-
> trial and military sabotage, labour agitation and strikes,
> continuous propaganda, terrorist acts against traitors and
> German leaders, boycotts and riots.
>
> . . . What is needed is a new organization to co-ordinate,
> inspire, control and assist nationals of the oppressed coun-
> tries who must themselves be the direct participants. We
> need absolute secrecy, a certain fanatical enthusiasm and
> willingness to work with people of different nationalities.

Dalton got his way, and on 16 July, 1940 Churchill formally
invited him to take charge of the new organisation. 'How
wonderful it would be if the Germans could be made to wonder
where they were going to be struck next, instead of forcing us to
try to wall in the Island and roof it over,' Churchill had
exclaimed when he approved the establishment of SOE.

The operations of SOE were so shrouded in secrecy that the general public did not know of its existence until the end of the war. It would be decades before the first government documents concerning the controversial organisation would be declassified and made available to the public, and even today some archives remain under lock and key in the vaults of the Public Record Office, while many were destroyed during and after the war.

SOE trained nationals from occupied countries (although there were many British agents too) in the arts of 'irregular warfare' before deploying them on specific missions. The work their operatives undertook was among the most dangerous of the conflict. They returned to their homelands as saboteurs, radio operators or resistance instructors, living in constant fear of being discovered and summarily executed.

SOE's existence was meant to be a secret to all but a few high-ranking officials in Whitehall and the military. To enter their London headquarters at 82 Baker Street in premises owned by Marks and Spencer, SOE chiefs arrived by a dark alley dressed in civilian clothes. (The Norwegian section was based a few hundred yards away at Chiltern Court, a mansion block above Baker Street Tube station.) The chiefs referred to themselves as the 'Org', the 'Racket' or the 'Old Firm'. Dozens of training schools were established up and down the country, mostly in remote country mansions, prompting the joke among British recruits that the initials SOE stood for 'Stately 'Omes of England'. (The Germans referred to SOE as the 'International School of Gangsters'.)

Following SOE's formation, a government memorandum defined its role and purpose as:

'A secret and independent organisation directed by the Minister of Economic Warfare for achieving the following purposes: to promote disaffection and, if possible, revolt in all enemy and enemy-occupied territories; to hamper the enemy's war effort by means of sabotage and 'partisan' warfare in those areas; to combat enemy interests and Fifth Column activities by 'unacknowledgeable' means and to create 'post-occupational organisations'.

SOE was at first bitterly resented by the chiefs of staff, who regarded it as a bunch of civilian amateurs who had never fired a shot in anger. There were plenty of men with military backgrounds on the operations side, but they were significantly outnumbered by the civilians at headquarters. Among them were bankers, academics, accountants, businessmen, wine traders, students, journalists, novelists, television and film producers and playwrights – virtually every branch of British professional life was represented.

The nature of SOE's work was held in contempt by the more reactionary generals, admirals, air marshals and other high-ranking officers, most of whom had seen action in the Great War. To these military 'purists' and moralists, guerrilla tactics were ungentlemanly and unsoldierly, promoting a mode of warfare completely out of keeping with the chivalrous traditions of the British services.

For the first two and a half years of its existence, the biggest challenge facing SOE was not operational but political. SIS, the Secret Intelligence Service, worked very closely with SOE, but they, more than any other department, felt uncomfortable about the plans and activities of their new partner. To SIS, SOE was a group of upstarts (they were right about that much), with little or no understanding or experience of secret operations, who were trespassing on their territory, in a political sense at home and in an operational sense abroad. SOE raids in occupied countries invariably led to a crackdown by the Gestapo, thus severely restricting the activities of the SIS agents, whose main business was to supply information about German troop and ship movements.

SOE may have been the pioneer of professional guerrilla warfare, but its reputation within Whitehall could not have been lower in the early part of 1942, when the urgency of destroying the raw materials of Hitler's atomic programme became apparent. The organisation, established just eighteen months earlier, was in the throes of growing pains as it set up its recruitment, training and planning programme while fighting skirmishes up and down the corridors of power in the capital. SOE received little sympathy or support as it struggled to construct a large-scale institution tasked with a wide-ranging brief with the bare minimum of resources. When the first Whitehall memorandum concerning the heavy water project in Vemork was transmitted to Major-General Colin Gubbins, the head of SOE, in the late spring of 1942, the organisation was presented with a perfect opportunity to prove itself in an operation of the highest importance.

Wrecking the stocks of heavy water had become an urgent priority, and Churchill himself began to take an active interest in the planning. The question of how that destruction could be achieved spawned dozens of meetings and hundreds of memos and telegrams between SOE, Combined Operations, the Norwegian government-in-exile, the War Office, the chiefs of staff, the Ministry of Economic Warfare, SIS and the Foreign

Office. The result was that plans for an attack became bogged in bureaucracy and riven by in-fighting. It was many months before the fog cleared, the power battles ceased and a decisive plan of action was finally drawn up. Throughout that period, Vemork's heavy water stocks were rising by the day, and Hitler's scientists were edging ever closer to building a weapon to end the Allies' fightback in a single, apocalyptic instant.

Attacking the Vemork plant was a strategic nightmare for the military planners. They could not count on any help from within as the Norwegian resistance movement barely existed as a significant force at the start of 1942. SOE did not have a single agent operating in the Telemark region. There was also the question of geography. The plant was situated 150 miles from Oslo and roughly the same distance from the nearest coastline, making it impossible to reach by any means except air. Up a narrow valley, accessible by just one road, Vemork was thought to be virtually impregnable as it jutted out of a cliff above a steep gorge and nestled at the foot of the Hardangervidda, the largest high-plateau wilderness in western Europe and home to some of the most inhospitable terrain and ferocious weather on the planet.

It was an extremely thorny political and diplomatic issue too. The blunderbuss approach favoured by some in the early stages of the planning entailed bombing the plant or the Møsvatn dam at the head of the valley. In a letter to Dr W. A. Akers at the Directorate of Tube Alloys (the harmless-sounding name given to Britain's atomic energy programme) within the Department of Scientific Industrial Research, his colleague Dr Perrin underlined the extent of Allied anxieties by mooting the possibility of such extreme measures.

You mentioned recently the question of attacking a hydro-electric plant from the air. It occurred to me that it might be a possible method to attack the reservoir, and I enclose some notes on the technical details. If you do not think this quite foolish you might care to pass it on to the right people and see what they say. It is evident that, if the method is possible, its use need not be questioned at the particular plant in question.

It was indeed a 'quite foolish' suggestion, although Perrin would not have been in a position to understand the consequences of the proposal. If the Møsvatn dam, holding back as it did a giant lake, was bombed, billions of gallons of water would have swept down the narrow valley for dozens of miles, wiping out every form of life in its way. In this area of Norway, everybody lived in towns and villages in the long valleys, but even those with houses higher up on their sunnier slopes – generally the better off – would have been swept to their death.

There was no hope that the Norwegian government-in-exile would ever agree to sanction the deaths of so many of its citizens, and indeed they immediately vetoed the idea. A major air assault on the plant itself was also fraught with danger as there was a risk that if a bomb were to hit one of the liquid-ammonia tanks at the plant, that too would have catastrophic consequences for the valley. A sabotage act carried out by a small party of commandos, meanwhile, presented a high risk not only to the soldiers involved, but also to the locals, who, it was feared, would suffer severe reprisals from the Germans, who would suspect that collaboration was involved.

'This is a very ticklish subject as you know and for various reasons has to be approved on a pretty high level before anything is done,' Colonel Jack Wilson, head of SOE's Norwegian section, told his colleagues. 'We have had a meeting with all the various authorities concerned and for reasons which have been explained to me and are valid, they agreed unanimously that the project suggested is undesirable and they are strongly opposed to any form of publicity in connection with the work involved.' 'They', we can assume, were the Norwegian authorities, while the 'project' was some form of bombing raid targeting either the dam or the plant.

The headlong rush to mount an operation was stopped in its tracks after one highly significant oversight by its planners – they had forgotten why Norway had come to be known as the 'land of the midnight sun'. The RAF needed the cover of darkness for most operations, but between April and November this dwindled to just a few hours a day in Scandinavia. Without it, the chances of being sighted and attacked by interceptor aircraft and anti-aircraft guns increased dramatically. A memo of May 1942, passed between the various departments involved in the planning, brought this obstacle to light:

> Figures at the disposal of the Air Ministry show that the area concerned there is now normally 18 hours of actual sunlight. To this must be added 1¼ hours at either end to allow for the twilight period and a further 40 minutes for height (of the aircraft). It will therefore be seen that for practical purposes there will only be some 2¼ hours of darkness available for the operation. The pin point is approximately 150 miles from the coast and to this must be added a further 50 miles in order to allow the aircraft to get out of the area in which fighter interception is likely.

Any attack on Vemork would thus have to bow to the laws of nature, and the planners would have to wait until the onset of winter. The delay did at least give the Allies time to sort out their differences and put together a concrete and detailed strategy for an assault. In July, following further discussions at the highest military and political levels, Norman Brook, an official at the War Cabinet Office, approached Combined Operations, now under the leadership of Lord Mountbatten, requesting them to weigh up the pros and cons of an attack.

> The Germans like ourselves are busy trying to split the atom in the belief that this will have a profound effect on H.E. [High Explosive] development and so win the war! It is established that they are using some fluid which they know as 'Heavy Water'. A source, perhaps the only one, from which they draw this is at Vemork near Rjukan on or near a large lake. Destruction of the source would considerably retard their investigations (perhaps). The source of production is in a deserted part of Norway . . . It might be a flying boat project. It may not be at all practicable but is it worth looking at.

The reply came back that it might be possible to send in paratroopers despite the mountainous, rugged terrain, but there would be little possibility of getting them out again as Vemork was so far from the nearest coastline. Officers at Combined Operations also warned against the use of gliders because of the terrain, and stated that it might be difficult to pinpoint the location from the air as the surrounding country was a bewildering landscape of similar-looking lakes and valleys. The only possible means of escape would be by flying boat. 'Surely this is a job for saboteurs with local knowledge?' they concluded.

While these rough plans were taking shape anxiety was starting to mount that news of Hitler's atomic bomb programme was in danger of leaking out to the general public. This was a scenario that the authorities were desperate to avoid at all costs, not least because British morale had been stretched to the limits of endurance by the Blitz and by mounting fears of Hitler's V-1 and V-2 rocket programmes. The prospect of London, the largest city on the planet, being razed to dust and rubble by a single bomb could spark mass panic amongst an already beleaguered population.

A 'Most Secret' SOE memo illustrates the concern.

> The application of this product [heavy water] to H.E. is both Churchill's and Hitler's real secret weapon, and bands of scientists are engaged in a race for the final result. Lately, the matter has been bandied about in a somewhat unofficial and unguarded manner between the War Office, C.C.O [Combined Operations] and ourselves. It is vitally necessary that the greatest secrecy should be preserved, and unfortunately many people appear to have been dabbling in this highly dangerous subject, without the slightest knowledge of its implications. . . . We are all agreed that neither of the terms given in my first sentence above should be used on paper or in conversation, hence the need for a code name.

The code name allocated for 'heavy water' was 'Lurgan,' and thereafter the very greatest secrecy surrounded the plans to destroy it. Not even those recruited to carry out the attack would be told what they were attempting to destroy.

Following reports that the Germans had ordered a further increase in the production of heavy water, an emergency meeting was held at the end of August 1942. Around the table were the two atomic scientists Dr Akers and Dr Perrin, Colonel Nevill of the Royal Marines, working with Combined Operations, and Professor Tronstad, working with SOE. The minutes of the meeting reported that they saw six possible courses of action:

1) Using men already employed at Vemork to blow up the stocks;
2) deploying agents to infiltrate the plant;
3) sending in an SOE sabotage party;
4) a Combined Operations attack using hydroplanes for arrival and departure;
5) sending in what they termed 'a suicide squad', i.e. one that had no chance of escaping afterwards;
6) RAF bombing.

All the options had their drawbacks. The use of an employee at the plant was an excellent idea in theory, but who could they get to carry out a task at such great risk not just to their own security, but also to that of their family? Tronstad suggested his friend and former colleague Brun, the new manager of the plant, but he was known from intelligence sources to be away from the Rjukan area at that time. SOE were cooler about the idea of infiltrating the plant with an agent from outside as this would still need cooperation from someone on the inside. SOE's position at this stage was that an attack by a small party of their own troops was possible, but there would be a far greater chance of success if a stronger force were deployed.

Significantly, SOE treated the Combined Operations and suicide missions as one and the same thing and were remarkably
dispassionate about the option, suggesting that if it was not possible to fly out the raiders then they could try to fight their way
the 400 kilometres to Sweden. How they would be expected to
do this in some of the most dangerous and inhospitable terrain
known to man while being pursued by the combined might of
the German Army, Luftwaffe and Gestapo, SOE did not make
clear. Bombing, they conceded, was certainly still a possibility
from a military point of view. Tronstad, however, was quick to
point out to his colleagues around the table that the Rjukan
valley was so narrow, deep and dark that precise bombing was
simply not feasible.

Over the summer, the planners came to the conclusion that the
only realistic form of attack was an SOE/Combined Operation.
An SOE telegram to Stockholm shortly after the meeting read:
'A's [General Hansteen's] instructions are for you to stop all plans
connected with B [Vemork plant]. Action will be taken from C
[Britain].' What we don't know is whether the 'plans' referred to
reconnaissance and intelligence for an aerial bombing raid or for
an altogether more extreme course of action, such as blowing up
the Møsvatn dam. But it was clear that such was the urgency of
the situation that the planners were prepared to consider every
single option, no matter how drastic.

2

Setting Europe Ablaze

In March 1942 those tasked with planning the attack on the heavy water stocks at Vemork enjoyed an extraordinary stroke of good fortune. A twenty-three-year-old Norwegian called Einar Skinnarland stepped off the *SS Galtesund* at Aberdeen after he and five other young patriots had seized the 600-ton coastal steamer and sailed it across the North Sea. Skinnarland was an engineer with contacts at the Vemork plant and lived with his brother Torstein next to the Møsvatn dam at the head of the valley. SOE, who did not have a single agent in the Telemark region at this time, could not have hoped to find a better recruit than this stocky, cheerful and resourceful character. A champion skier and a fine outdoorsman, Skinnarland was born and raised in the area and knew everyone in the local community. Crucially, he had a string of reliable contacts inside the plant who would be able to supply him with a stream of vital information about German plans and progress. He had seven brothers and sisters living in and around the Rjukan area, and they too, especially Torstein, were dedicated to the resistance cause.

Skinnarland, who told his employers that he was taking his annual holiday, was put through an intensive SOE training course in a wide range of operational activities, including W/T

(Wireless/Telegraph), explosives and intelligence-gathering. On the night of 28/29 March 1942, just eleven days after arriving in Scotland, he was dropped back into Telemark by parachute, with the brief to gather as much information as possible about German activities at Vemork.

Skinnarland, like so many of his compatriots, had led a peaceful, simple existence before the German's blitzkrieg, but it is a testament to his spirit that he threw himself into the cause with the bare minimum of training behind him. He was given just one dummy parachute drop before the night of his return. The drop was a hair-raising experience for him and the six RAF crew on the Whitley that took off from Kinloss that evening. The pilots had no problem locating the dropping zone, but when they arrived there Skinnarland, the most courageous of operators on the ground, suffered a panic attack at the critical moment and refused to jump, causing alarm among the crew, who were eager to make their drop and get out of enemy airspace as quickly as possible.

He was sitting with his feet dangling out of the bottom of the plane, the freezing wind yanking at his legs and the noise of the engines roaring in his ears. Below him lay the frozen, remote mountains and lakes of his homeland. It was a terrifying experience. Even seasoned paratroopers still feel the fear of dropping: the tightening of the stomach muscles, the surge of adrenalin and the frantic beating of the heart. We can only imagine what it must have been like for a man who, until a few days earlier, had never flown in an aeroplane, let alone jump out of one into one of the most inhospitable environments on earth with only a thin silk sheet and a few strings standing between him and death.

In the operational report, the dispatcher responsible for over-seeing Skinnarland's drop wrote: 'On receiving green light, tried to get passenger to jump but at first he refused, and made several counter suggestions, all contradictory. He did not want to put his legs through the hole, and showed very little taste for his job. The aircraft flew backwards and forwards for 20 minutes before he was induced to jump on being told that the a/c [aircraft] could not fly any longer.'

The following morning Skinnarland turned up to work and cheerfully told his colleagues at the plant that he had had enjoyed a relaxing break. No one suspected that he had actually spent his holiday capturing a German ship and being trained in the dark arts of guerrilla warfare. The role of the Skinnarland brothers in the unfolding story cannot be overstated. Both men took excep-tional risks in collecting intelligence for London and providing vital equipment and assistance for the advance party that would arrive later in the year. All SOE agents in Norway were given the codenames of birds and Einar Skinnarland was to be known as Grouse.

The ten-day course Skinnarland underwent at SOE's Norwegian training centre in the Highlands of Scotland was a highly condensed version of what his compatriots, several of them known to him, were being put through by SOE in dozens of Special Trainings Schools (STS) up and down the country throughout that summer. They were all volunteers of the Norwegian Independent Company, known as the Linge Company after a Norwegian soldier, Captain Martin Linge, who was killed by a German sniper during a commando land-ing in December 1941.

The training programme was as wide ranging, comprehensive and intense as any ever undertaken by a military power. Those who made it through the gruelling course would be formidable operators in the field, capable of withstanding the greatest physical stress and mental pressure that the rigours of war can present. They would also be highly skilled in a number of diverse areas, such as close combat and silent killing, industrial sabotage, W/T, intelligence-gathering, propaganda and outdoor survival in extreme conditions. In SOE, you needed brains in equal measure to brawn.

All the young Norwegians who had risked their lives to escape to Britain to join the war effort had already marked themselves out as men of great bravery and ingenuity. Those who made it through SOE's heavy vetting process and intensive training programme were men of even higher calibre. Many of them had been in Britain for over a year, and they were starting to get restless. It was over two years since the German invasion of their homeland, and it was not to enjoy the beauty of the Scottish Highlands or the stately homes of England that they had put their lives on the line to escape occupation. The training had been first class and the British had been generous hosts, but their lust for combat and desire to liberate their compatriots were mounting by the week.

During that summer of 1942, SOE's instructors began to scour the Norwegian ranks for a handful of exceptional 'students' capable of preparing and leading one of the most daring sabotage acts in the history of warfare. These could not be ordinary soldiers, no matter how tough, fit, intelligent and well trained. They also had to be outdoorsmen of the highest order, men from the mountains, who knew how to cope with the most demanding challenges nature could offer.

It was from the ranks of the elite Linge Company that ten men were singled out over the coming months to play a part in attacking the Vemork heavy water plant: Jens Anton Poulsson, Arne Kjelstrup, Knut Haukelid, Claus Helberg, Knut Haugland, Joachim Rønneberg, Birger Strømsheim, Hans Storhaug, Kasper Idland and Fredrik Kayser. They were just names on a list in 1942, eager young recruits like hundreds of thousands of others. But within nine months that list was sitting on the desk of Winston Churchill in 10 Downing Street.

While Britain's leading military planners argued among themselves about how best to launch a raid on Vemork, SOE had a small advance party ready to be dropped into the Rjukan area to pave the way for an attack. Poulsson, an experienced mountaineer, was chosen as its leader, and he had picked out Haukelid, Helberg, Haugland and Kjelstrup to form the original party, to be known as Operation Grouse.

Poulsson was a distinctive figure with his giant frame and a pipe permanently stuck in the corner of his mouth. His journey to England had been a dramatic adventure in itself. Norway is just 400 miles from Britain, and most volunteers arrived in small fishing vessels – on a route that came to be known as The 'Shetland bus'. Poulsson, though, had to travel halfway around the world via four continents. After escaping to Sweden he was unable to get directly to the UK as there were no flights between the two countries in early 1941, so he went to Finland, and from there over the border into the Soviet Union and south to Turkey. Unable to find a boat to take him through the Mediterranean and north to Britain, he travelled through Syria, Lebanon, Palestine and Egypt, from where he took a boat to India and then to South Africa before boarding another heading across the Atlantic to Trinidad. From the Caribbean he flew to Canada, where he was given passage on one of the regular convoys back across the Atlantic. Nine months after he set out from Norway, he finally arrived at Liverpool docks in October and immediately enlisted with the Norwegian forces.

Poulsson had stood out as a fine soldier during the SOE training, but he had other qualities too. He was from Rjukan, and as a young boy he had watched the giant Vemork hydroelectric plant being constructed just a few miles from his family home. He loved the outdoors and had spent much of his childhood and early manhood living out on the Hardangervidda, the great wilderness on Rjukan's doorstep. He was regarded by his peers as an excellent 'hillman', who relished life up on the frozen wastes of the wild plateau close to his home. Poulsson's parents, two sisters and brother were living in Rjukan at the time, but when he was chosen to lead the advance party operation he was placed under strict orders not to have any contact with his family.

Haukelid, meanwhile, was singled out in his SOE training reports as a man of outstanding qualities: 'Intelligent, keen, works very hard. An exceptionally efficient NCO, who is a good leader. He is a cool and calculating type, who should give a very good account of himself in a tight corner. A hard worker. A really sound man and cunning. Has no fear. Another excellent student who would do well in almost any special job. Might fit several categories.'

Gubbins, the SOE chief, described him as 'a hunter, philosopher and man of action'. Born in New York in 1911 but raised in Norway, Haukelid had worked in an Oslo-based company importing machinery before hostilities broke out. He took a job in a German submarine base in Trondheim at the start of the war, passing valuable information to a resistance wireless operator, but after the telegraphist was caught by the Gestapo he fled to Sweden and then to England.

Helberg was another native of Rjukan and had sat next to Poulsson in the town's little school. He had joined the Norwegian Mountaineering Club, but when war broke out in Europe he decided to undergo military training. He had spent just eighty-four days in the army when the Germans invaded, and after seven days of fighting north of Oslo he was captured and sent to a makeshift prisoner-of-war camp. He escaped and returned to his job at the mountaineering association before fleeing to Stockholm, where he volunteered to undertake intelligence work after a meeting with Major Malcolm Munthe of SOE.

At a time when there were no W/T operators at work in the country, Helberg's task was to smuggle messages across the Swedish frontier from where they would be delivered to London. It was via this smuggling route that the Allies had learned of German plans to increase the production of heavy water at Vemork. During one mission he was arrested by a Swedish border guard, convicted and spent a total of four months in prison either side of his trial. On his release, the British and Norwegian authorities in Stockholm arranged for him to be flown to the UK, where he immediately enlisted in the Linge Company. Like all the men chosen for the Grouse operation, Helberg was an astounding outdoorsman as well as a champion Nordic skier. He was a colourful character with a tendency to take great risks and land himself in the deepest trouble, only to extricate himself from it with the bluff of a great actor and the cool bravado of a true adventurer.

Haugland was a W/T operator of the very highest quality. He had been a radio operator on a merchantman before the war and had taken part in the rearguard action that had followed the German invasion. Following the occupation he took a job in a radio factory and began working for the resistance, but after being arrested three times he escaped to England via Sweden and joined the Linge Company.

Kjelstrup was born in Rjukan but raised in the Oslo area. He had spent a lot of time in the Telemark region during the winters and could look after himself in the harshest of conditions as well as anyone. Poulsson had met him on the boat from Canada and was instantly impressed by the man. He was small but powerfully built, a plumber with a great sense of humour and a man who loved a fight. During the German invasion of Norway he had shown his courage and daring when, together with just one other patriot, he had attacked a whole German column advancing up-country – another man for a tight corner.

By the time the men of the Grouse advance party had been chosen, SOE had become a micro-society with its own industry, laws and culture. To recruit and train agents, a huge infrastructure had been created out of nothing, an especially daunting enterprise given the privations of the day. Training schools, research institutions and various headquarters up and down the country had to be established. Factories were converted for the production of special equipment, including weapons, wireless sets designed for covert use, forged documents, clothing and countless other accessories.

In most cases prospective agents were seconded to SOE by the military or the government-in-exile of their country. Like all recruits, the men of the Grouse party and their compatriots in the Linge Company underwent a vetting process at the Royal Victoria 'Patriotic School' on Wandsworth Common in London. They were told only vaguely how they would be employed if they qualified, and they were made to sign a document relating to the Official Secrets Act, which forbade them to discuss SOE with anyone, even the officers in the unit from which they came. It was at this stage that the outstanding talents could be spotted and most of the undesirables removed – it was surprising, given the desperate need for recruits, how ruthless SOE were in culling the numbers.

Recruitment officers used their professional judgement and common sense when it came to picking suitable candidates for SOE. The American equivalent, OSS, followed a rigid formula neatly laid out in official guides, but it was full of abstract and woolly definitions and psychiatric profiling. SOE recruiters preferred to trust their instincts, and they deployed a number of devious techniques to weed out the unsuitable candidates.

Throughout the training the behaviour of the Norwegian 'students' was covertly scrutinised by observers to try to catch out those not up to the mark. In apparently informal settings, they were offered strong drink, first to see how much they could take and then to see how they reacted when they were under the influence. Those who started blabbing or became indiscreet or aggressive were immediately sent back to their units. They were even watched at night to see whether they talked in their sleep and risked blowing their identity. (The bedrooms of British recruits, who were all fluent in the language of the country to which they were to be sent, were infiltrated by observers to see whether they sleep-talked in English.)

SOE had established sixty Special Training Schools (STS), most of them in Britain but with some in North Africa and Italy for Mediterranean and eastern European operations. Each STS specialised in a particular area of training or housed the nationals of a given country. By the end of the war 7,500 operatives had been sent out into western Europe from Britain and 4,000 from the Mediterranean; 700 of them would be dead.

The training programme was established by Colonel Jack Wilson, and by the time he had transferred to take over SOE's Norwegian section in 1942 there existed a flourishing network of specialist schools, producing agents and guerrilla warriors of the very highest pedigree.

The men of Operation Grouse were taught how to set up a base, recruit and train more agents to form paramilitary units, arrange for the dropping of supplies and arrival of other agents or troops, establish intelligence contacts, plan and execute sabotage operations and acquire a basic understanding of W/T operations.

Following their selection the Norwegians were sent on a three-week preliminary course for physical fitness, map reading and weapons training. They were then transferred to the schools in the Highlands and/or the west coast of Scotland for more advanced programmes and more intensive survival training before heading back to England for parachute instruction and tuition in specialised areas such as communications or propaganda.

Communication between the Grouse party and their SOE masters was a vital part of the operation. In 1942 SOE was allowed to break from the Secret Intelligence Service and set up its own communications network, enabling it to use its own coding systems and communicate directly with its agents in the field. SOE's two main communications centres were based at Poundon in Oxfordshire and Grendon Underwood in Buckinghamshire, staffed by FANYs (First Aid Nursing Yeomanry), and it was through them that Skinnarland and the Grouse party passed back vital intelligence. A curious intimacy between the agents in the field and the FANYs was established, and many of the longer-serving women were able to recognise the identity of the agent by the rhythm and style of his trans-missions. The Norwegians, like so many SOE operatives, devel-oped a great fondness for the FANYs, who performed a wide range of other activities for the organisation. 'I am tongue-tied when I try to tell what the FANYs have meant to the organisa-tion and me,' said SOE chief Gubbins. 'They were everything and without them we just could not have done it. They have become a household word for guts, efficiency, cheerfulness, per-sistence, tenacity and comradeship in difficulty. They have been magnificent and invaluable.'

In the other national sections within SOE many of the opera-tives dropped behind enemy lines were British, but the Norwegian unit was exclusively made up of people from that country, for the simple reason that it was virtually impossible to find a Briton who looked and sounded exactly like a Norwegian. The agents had to be able to pass themselves off as locals if they came into contact with the enemy or the local population. Furthermore, there were very few Britons available at the time who could survive the ferocious conditions of a Norwegian winter in the wild. The Norwegians, steeped in the traditions of survival and snowcraft of their forefathers, knew how to cope with the extremities of their climate and the hostility of their environment.

The Norwegians trained in the Highlands of Scotland, where the terrain most closely approximated to the wilds of their homeland and offered the only place in Britain where they could practise cross-country skiing for significant periods of the year. A giant area of Scotland, everywhere north of an imaginary line between Fort William and Inverness, was set aside for training and designated a Protected Area. This remote region was easily closed off and was extremely difficult for enemy spies to penetrate. There was also a host of good-sized houses and lodges to accommodate the recruits, as well as a wide variety of terrain, including mountains, marshes, coastline, lochs and rivers. A number of other areas farther south on the west coast and in the Cairngorms were also set aside.

The Norwegian station was known as STS 26 and was housed at Drumintoul and Glenmore, Victorian shooting lodges near Aviemore in the foothills of the Cairngorms. It is a stunning, secluded setting close to a loch teeming with trout and streams full of salmon, nestling within the ancient pine woods of Rothiemurchus in which deer abound. Those who passed through STS 26 and survived the war retained the warmest memories of this beautiful place and the generosity of the inhabitants. Some of the local ghillies and gamekeepers, however, took longer to be won over by the Norwegians, who liked to supplement their army rations by helping themselves to the abundant local produce on offer. Helberg was once caught stealing salmon by a local gamekeeper and was hauled before the SOE instructors to explain himself. 'My officers were very annoyed –

not that I was poaching salmon, but that I was caught!' he recalled. On other occasions, the Norwegians resorted to less traditional methods, hurling grenades into the water to land their catch.

The SOE Norwegian section enrolled around twenty to twenty-five men a month for the first three years following its formation. In the Highlands and on the west coast this band of young men learned to live and operate in rough, hostile terrain, to avoid walking on the skyline, to crawl silently through bush and scrub, to condition their bodies to withstand deep fatigue and stress, to cross rivers and streams and climb cliffs. The Grouse advance party, like many of their compatriots, were already familiar with some of these practices, but the training still served to prime and toughen them up for the challenges that lay ahead. The fieldcraft element of the course also involved map reading and compass work and teaching the recruits to memorise routes so that they could find their way by day or night without any aids. They also underwent exercises in the use of explosives, blowing up dummy targets. (One of the instructors in the Highlands was Gavin Maxwell, who wrote the best-selling *Ring of Bright Water*, the book about otters.)

'The outdoor training in Scotland from my point of view was very easy. Since I was a small boy, my main interest had been the outdoor life: hunting, fishing and living out in the mountains,' Poulsson recalled. 'So the training in the Cairngorms and other places in Scotland was actually a pleasure for me. The other training we got in England was very, very important but no one in England was going to tell me how to take care of men or how to live in the mountains.'

After the physical training programme and instruction in explosives and weaponry, the Norwegians were sent to other STS throughout England for specialist training in signals and industrial sabotage. At the end of the programme, Grouse had to undergo the dreaded parachute training course at STS 51 at Ringwood in the Greater Manchester area, where they were made to jump off high platforms, told how to roll properly and were dragged at speed along the ground at the end of a long rope. At the conclusion of the course they were made to parachute in the dark from a balloon just 1,500 feet in the air. Those who refused to jump were removed from the course. This was a terrifying experience for the men, worse than jumping from a plane because the chute opened after five seconds rather than just two and you fell directly to earth rather than being pulled along almost horizontally by the wind. This, the men of Grouse agreed, was by far the most challenging aspect of their training. All British airborne troops learned the craft at Ringway, and by the end of the war 60,000 had passed through its doors and jumped from its balloons, including the Red Berets of the British Airborne Commandos.

SOE training involved all the basic elements given to regular infantrymen in the British Army, plus extensive coaching in the practices of 'irregular' warfare: blowing safes, breaking locks, laying explosives and booby traps, close-combat fighting with knives, chloroform, poison, fists and boots. These were not the conventional practices of the honourable warrior, but the rules and conventions of warfare had changed.

At Aston House in Hertfordshire recruits were trained in the arts of silent killing, unarmed combat and small-arms use by, among others, two former Shanghai policemen called Eric 'Bill'

Sykes and William Fairbairn. They were both great characters, remembered with a mixture of fondness and fear by their students. Sykes liked to tell them that he would show them how to use a knife as 'delicately as an artist with a paintbrush'.

Sykes and Fairbairn became names well known throughout military circles for their design of the British Commando knife, which was to become a standard weapon in the Second World War and for decades to follow. Using their experience in close-quarters combat, the pair designed a weapon based on an ancient Egyptian model intended to strike accurately at a target's vital organs. It was perfectly balanced for throwing, but with twin cutting edges its main purpose was as a thrusting weapon.

Sykes was reputed to have possessed 'the fastest draw in the Far East' while working with the sniper unit of the Shanghai police, capable of drawing his pistol from its shoulder holster, cocking the gun and hitting his target in under a second. Sykes and Fairbairn instructed their students in the use of the Sten carbine gun and automatic pistols, which were either .32 or .45 calibre. One of the methods developed by Sykes was called 'instinctive' shooting (firing without aiming) and was later adopted and adapted by the army.

Another trainer, Harry Court, instructed the recruits never to kill a German, but to try to hospitalise him for six months, saying he was more of a nuisance alive than dead because his rehabilitation tied up German manpower and resources. 'He's no good to us in the ground,' he would say. Other instructors, however, urged their students to kick a man to death. Court also taught the recruits how to break a man's jaw with the heel of their hand rather than the knuckles – a technique he favoured

37

because there was no risk of breaking their own bones. Court also liked to point out that a man always had a lethal weapon somewhere about his person in the form of a pen, a metal comb or an umbrella.

Demolition training was provided by explosives experts, engineers and architects, who taught recruits the most effective and economical ways of destroying factories, houses, barracks, bridges, dams, trains, gates, reservoirs, port installations, railway lines and ships.

At the end of the course the Norwegians, like all SOE students, were sent to 'finishing school', the biggest of which was at Beaulieu, the stately home of Lord Montagu in the New Forest, which now houses the National Motor Museum. It was here they learned some of the finer points about operations in the field, such as coding, microphotography, establishing local contacts, use of couriers, preparation of dropping zones (DZs), creation of false documents and how to avoid capture. They were also shown how to hide microfilm on their bodies, usually up the backside, and what to do if they were being interrogated by the Gestapo. These interrogation sessions were highly realistic and terrifying. Short of actual torture, the acting Gestapo officer, complete with rasping German accent, would employ every other means of extracting information, including shining a bright light in their faces, screaming in their ears and smashing steel rods down on the table.

Thus it was that, three months after walking through the door of the 'Patriotic School' in Wandsworth, recruits had been transformed from ordinary laymen or foot soldiers into highly trained killers and secret agents, ready, as Churchill had put it, to 'set Europe ablaze'.

When the Grouse party had completed their various training programmes they were handed a wad of pound notes and sent to London to buy their own cold-weather gear. They knew better than anyone the type of conditions they would face in a Norwegian winter, and it was only sensible that they should choose the equipment that would help keep them alive when the temperature plunged to minus 30 degrees Celsius with a wind-chill factor that would make it feel twice as cold. They went first to the famous sports store Lillywhites near Piccadilly Circus, a popular shop among Britain's army of amateur outdoor adventurers in peacetime. Operating under the privations of war, though, Lillywhites were unable to provide the type of gear appropriate for living in the Norwegian wilderness.

For most of their equipment, the party went to a Norwegian army supply shop in Dumfries, where they were kitted out with gloves, balaclavas and ski boots to supplement the kit provided by SOE. Nordic skis and boots, essential prerequisites for any operation conducted during the Norwegian winter, came from a supplier in Iceland and from a store of goods donated by the many Norwegians who had fled to Scotland after the outbreak of hostilities. The most important aspect of their personal equipment was the sleeping bag, which had to provide maximum warmth and water resistance and roll into as small a size as possible.

At this point in the war British resources were being stretched to the limit. Germany's U-boat campaign had severely undermined the flow of supply ships bringing vital cargo to Britain's shores. Strict rationing had long been in place for the civilian population, and factories were struggling to keep up with the intense demand for military equipment. The United States had only recently joined the Allied war effort, and their largesse, which was to play so great a part in the defeat of Nazi Germany and Imperial Japan, was yet to have a significant impact on Britain's own efforts.

The Linge Company was by no means the only unit of the Allied war machine to feel a mounting sense of frustration at the lack of resources and concrete operational plans that conspired to restrain them in the first part of 1942. Starved of information and equipment, and apparently of any immediate prospects of going into action, the newly trained recruits became restless. The desperation of the advance party to play some part in the war against the occupiers of their homeland boiled over in June, when they wrote a letter to Major Munthe at SOE, complaining that they were being ignored and threatening to transfer to the regular Norwegian Army in exile. Munthe's reply attempted to reassure them, but warned them that they would miss out on the best action if they decided to leave.

I beg you not to listen too trustingly to the many persons who are only too willing to spread rumours, which are usually in no way founded on fact . . . I would like to remind you that no matter however much you and I may try to obtain facilities for extra training, we must face the possibility of continued delay, since this little group in which you and I are so interested is only a very small part of the vast army of 2,000,000 men sitting on these Islands making exactly the same complaints, all of them as you are making, and all of them anxious to be given something active to do or further active training. Doesn't it strike you that every weapon which is given to you for training purposes is one

less weapon sent into the field against the Germans? . . .
Though you may have a week or 10 days of fresh interest if
you join the Norwegian Army and leave the Linge
Company, you will very soon find yourself in the same position of boredom.

As autumn approached and the nights started to grow longer in
Scandinavia, SOE decided that they would send in the advance
party. The rough plan at this stage was for Grouse to act as a
reception committee for British airborne troops. They would
carry out reconnaissance missions and then guide in the aircraft
and lead the British commandos to the plant, acting as part of a
covering party or fighting force if necessary. But the group had a
longer-term objective too, to organise and train guerrilla detachments in the Telemark region independently of the resistance
movement Milorg, with which they were instructed to avoid all
contact so as not to compromise their operations. The less a man
knew, the less he could give away under interrogation. During
their training, the SOE instructors had been at pains to impress
upon their students the importance of ensuring that any resistance groups they created remained deep underground until the
order from London for them to rise up was given. If they were to
take the fighting out into the open in the mistaken belief that an
Allied invasion was imminent, then the Norwegian resistance
movement, such as it was, would be wiped out, the Allies would
be back to square one and the cause of Norwegian liberation
from tyranny would be set back for years.

'In doing this training, it should be made quite clear that this
is not a sign of immediate invasion. On the contrary,' their orders
stressed. Strict limits on their activities were imposed by SOE.

The groups would be allowed to attack German telegraph and telephone communications, bridges and road passes connecting eastern and western Telemark, as well as prominent Hirdmen (the Norwegian equivalent of the SS) or 'denouncers' working secretly for the Germans. Grouse would be issued with machine guns, pistols, grenades and explosives, but they were also given the means to kill silently as the following internal SOE memo makes clear: 'Since the Grouse men have been equipped, the most important of the poisons, "U", has become available and it has been suggested that they be equipped with it. We therefore suggest six doses with one syringe only.'

Any militia groups they trained were to be no larger than about ten men and, if possible, only the leaders of the groups should know each other. Balaclavas were to be worn at all meetings between members so that in the event of capture and interrogation by the Gestapo the identity of their comrades would not be revealed.

Skinnarland had informed SOE that there were roughly a hundred Germans stationed at Rjukan, a fifteen minute drive to the plant at Vemork, around another twenty billeted near his house at the Møsvatn dam, fifteen minutes in the other direction, with another thirty-five billeted in a school close to the plant and around twenty inside the complex itself. He also confirmed that three iron hawsers had been stretched across the valley to prevent low-flying bombers from attacking the plant, but the precise number and position of AA guns in the area were not known. Skinnarland had also heard through his contacts that the Germans were preparing to lay landmines around the giant water pipes that fed the Hydro plant from the steep precipice behind.

As soon as possible Grouse were to establish wireless stations and arrange dropping points for the supply of arms and other equipment and the passing on of intelligence regarding their activities and those of the Germans. They were all issued with false names and faked identity and ration cards. Haugland and Helberg would be students, Poulsson a mechanic and Kjelstrup a *rørlegger* (plumber).

Skinnarland would be informed of their imminent arrival at a prearranged rendezvous, a hut in the hills up on the Hardanger-vidda plateau, via a covert message read out on the BBC Norwegian news service on the night the operation should be expected. The announcer would say 'This is the latest news from London' rather than the usual 'This is the news from London'. When it arrived the party was to make contact with Einar's brother, Torstein, at the Møsvatn dam where he worked. The party member would use the password 'Do you know Auntie Kjersti?' to which Torstein would reply: 'No, but I know her brother.' If possible, Skinnarland was to put out lights at the dropping place to guide in the RAF plane.

Knut Haukelid was earmarked to play a central role in the advance party, but an accident in training in which he shot him-self through the foot led to his withdrawal. It was a devastating blow for the young officer, who, like the others, was itching to get back to Norway and see some action.

The whole party were deeply frustrated by the long delay in their deployment caused either by unsuitable weather conditions or technical problems. By the end of the summer they had been thoroughly trained in every area of covert special operation work and had spent months sitting on their kit waiting for the order to stand by. Their irritation and feeling of helplessness mounted as each boring day merged into the next. Twice they packed their kit and headed to the aerodrome near Wick, having been told that their hour had finally come.

Southern Norway lay within striking distance for the RAF, but the weather and the lie of the land made parachute dropping and glider-borne operations a highly hazardous exercise. The country's long coastline was excellent for amphibious or naval-led operations, and although its great wilderness inland gave planes a greater chance of avoiding detection, the broken terrain, maze of lakes and endless expanse of snow and ice made the pinpointing of locations difficult. For the RAF, who played a major and heroic role in the Norway theatre, it was as tough as assignments came, not least because the coastline had been heavily fortified with anti-aircraft guns after Hitler had become convinced that Churchill and Roosevelt had decided to launch their planned invasion on occupied Europe through this Scandinavian country.

On each occasion the plane carrying Grouse had reached the Norwegian coast but was forced to turn back, the first time because cloud made it impossible for them to find the dropping zone and the second because engine trouble left the pilots no choice but to abandon the mission. To have come so close only to be disappointed at the final moment represented a heavy test of the Norwegians' nerve. As they had stood by in their Scottish safe house, the adrenalin had been steadily rising, and by the time the plane had crossed the North Sea the four men had reached a fever pitch of fear and excitement. The sense of anti-climax they felt as the plane began to bank and head back to Scotland was overwhelming for the young patriots primed for action.

Each day spent in Britain was one day lost in the fight to liberate their compatriots from Nazi tyranny. They were, in a sense, prisoners of war, restrained from fighting for their cause. A series of letters written to the convalescent Haukelid by Poulsson on behalf of the advance party illustrates their exasperation during this waiting period. For much of the time, they were moved from one safe house to the next and entertained by FANYs, who did their best to take the soldiers' minds off the interminable wait. But there was only so much they could do to alleviate the boredom.

Giving his address as 'Somewhere in England', Poulsson wrote:

> If you think we have left you are damned wrong. Today is Sunday, and we came here last Monday. A week's waiting for fine weather which never comes. Otherwise it is alright here – the house full of FANYs.
>
> 12th Sept: There is Red Light today and we hope for the best. We are now ready to start!
>
> 27th Sept: Of course we came back. Motor trouble. We have now been here four weeks, but today, Sunday, we are going to try again.
>
> 28th Sept: Another unsuccessful attempt. Fog in the North Sea. Devil take the lot! But tails up.

Such was their boredom that Poulsson and Helberg even wrote some poetry to pass the time and amuse the hobbling Haukelid, but even these light-hearted pieces express a sense of their hopelessness. The following was composed by Helberg at the end of September, when the party had just about reached the end of their tethers:

Have you seen them, the lads
They who rush through the air,
The heroes from Piccadilly,
Ever more than willing
To offer life and limb
For their soldier friends.

But now they have lost their splendour
All have stopped their dance
Depression rules the boys
For they were the Commandos' drudges.
But now they can only bluff
Over deeds of a by-gone time.
They got 30,000 for the jobs
And that the lads couldn't stand.

(They had been given NOK 30,000 to finance illegal activities in Norway.) The young Norwegian's lyrical efforts convey the despair of the party as they twiddled their thumbs in Britain's country houses and shooting lodges.

On the night of 18 October 1942, the Grouse party once again boarded the RAF Halifax bomber and took off for Norway.

3

Long Day's Journey into Night

It was a clear evening as the four Grouse men took their seats and Wing Commander Hockey and Flight Lieutenant Sutton lifted their Halifax into the skies above the North Sea just after seven o'clock. It took over four hours for the bomber to reach their designated dropping zone, but this time the weather held as they approached the Telemark region and began a steep descent for the drop. It was a clear bright night, and below them the saboteurs could see the rugged earth of their homeland. They could make out long winding fjords and lakes, twisted among the steep narrow valleys and low, snow-covered mountain peaks. They could also see the lights of homes and vehicles, some of them perhaps belonging to their friends and family. What had become of them over the past year or two? Were they alive? Were they in concentration camps? The return would be particularly strange for Poulsson, Haugland and Helberg, who would be camped up on the frozen desert of the Hardangervidda, just a few kilometres from where they were brought up and where their families were still living. Or at least they hoped they were.

The Hardangervidda, 3,500 square miles of almost entirely uninhabited wilderness, was set, as winter approached, to become a forbidding, frozen wasteland for the following six months. The Hardanger is a mass of rock, lakes, rivers and streams, an environment too harsh for most vegetation and animals. Reindeer, grouse, ptarmigan and the odd snowy fox can be found, but humans come there at their peril in winter.

To fly over the Hardangervidda is a breathtaking experience. Today, as then, on a clear day, it looks like a polar ice cap or the very far north of Canada, stretching as far as the eye can see. The only signs of human life are a handful of hunters' huts, most of which are situated along the shores of the lakes. There, on the lower reaches, are glades of birch trees, but higher up there is simply nothing. The rest is just snow, rock and ice. From the air a herd of several hundred reindeer look like no more than a handful of dots on a giant white canvas. The sight of the Hardangervidda from the air fills onlookers with a sense of awe in ordinary circumstances, but for the Grouse party that night, returning to the land of their fathers to fight for its freedom, it must have been an especially humbling and breathtaking experience.

The Hardangervidda is a place people choose to visit, but where only a small hardy handful can live. When the Germans invaded Norway they went *around* it, and when their troops were dispatched to search it for resistance fighters or phantom British paratroopers, they never ventured farther than half a day's march so that they could be sure of getting off it by nightfall. To the Germans it was a dreadful place, a frozen hell. But for the four members of the Grouse party, it was about to become home.

As they approached the dropping zone, Sergeant Hill, the RAF dispatcher, opened the hatch in the floor of the plane. It was time to jump. The hearts of the four young soldiers began to thump even harder with a mixture of fear and exhilaration. Their war was about to begin. The four of them stood in line, wearing jumping gear and laden with equipment, as the freezing wind rushed into the plane out of the darkness. At 2318 hours, Sergeant Hill hurled the first of six containers holding their supplies and then, one after the other, the men jumped in rapid succession. Poulsson went first, followed by Haugland, Kjelstrup and then Helberg.

None of them had any control over what happened in those next few seconds. Their chutes were attached to a line inside the aircraft, which after 16 feet of their fall would start to rip the silk chute out of the rucksack on their backs. It was vital that there should be no hesitation between the jumpers because the plane was travelling at about 200 feet per second. The maths were simple: if you dawdled for a moment or two you would find yourself landing hundreds of yards away from your comrades and in danger of missing the dropping zone. But all four of them jumped as the dispatcher ordered them to, between one and two seconds after their predecessor.

'I think we were all nervous when we were jumping through the hole in the bottom of the aircraft – at least I certainly was – but then it was a very happy feeling to see Norway coming up to greet us,' Poulsson later recollected.

Hill hurled out two more packages and quickly slammed the hatch shut. As the plane prepared to bank before starting its gauntlet run back home, they could see twelve parachutes, framed by the bright moonlight and in perfect symmetrical order, descending in a diagonal line to the rough snow-speckled terrain below. Wing Commander Hockey wrote in his operation report: 'Exact pinpoint found and load dropped as one stick. . . . Load dropped from 700–1000ft flying due south (down wind in view of nature of ground and moon). Snow only seen on high ground.' The dispatcher reported: 'Men jumped well and without hesitation.' The reargunner observed: '12 chutes seen to open and all men to land with exception of last package.'

What the crew couldn't see as they set off to drop thousands of propaganda leaflets around Stavanger before heading out to the North Sea was the mighty thump with which the Norwegians and their equipment hit the rough ground. 'It was fortunate that none of us was severely hurt when we landed,' Poulsson recorded in his log. 'The ground was just a mass of stones.' The four ripped off their parachutes as soon they hit the ground, knowing full well that a crosswind could drag them across the rugged terrain, tearing their flesh and breaking their bones. Helberg hurt himself in the landing and it would be a week before he recovered fully.

For the next four hours the party searched for the eight containers and packages upon which their mission and immediate survival depended. A combination of darkness and the broken terrain made this near impossible, and at 0400 hours they decided to call it a night and continue their search by daylight. They spent that first night close to where they landed, huddled in sleeping bags behind a large rock formation as shelter from the wind. Just as they were about to settle down for the night, Poulsson sat the other three down and told them the true purpose of their mission: that they were to act as a guiding party for a unit of British commandos tasked to blow up the heavy water plant at Vemork.

'I was told by Colonel Wilson before leaving for Norway that the operation was very important because the Germans could blow up a part of London if they got hold of heavy water,' recalled Poulsson. 'I didn't have a clue what heavy water was and I didn't believe him.' It is important to remember that for the generation brought up after the First World War it was very difficult to imagine any explosive power greater than a 500-pound bomb fired by a giant artillery gun or dropped from one of the new types of long-range aircraft that had recently come into service.

It took the party two days of exhausting wading through 'wet' snow to collect all the equipment that was scattered across the rugged hillside. Each man set off in different directions to search for the containers submerged in the snowdrifts or hidden between rocks. One of the reasons it took so long was because their skiing equipment was in the last of the containers they found. Had they found it first they could have been on their way within a few hours. In these conditions, you can barely operate without skis.

The weather was fine during those forty-eight hours, but they were surprised to discover where they were once they were able to identify their position. They had landed on a mountainside east of Fjarefit in the Songadalen, 10 miles west of where they were meant to land on marshes east of Ugleflott, which in turn was about 20 miles from Vemork. Under normal circumstances covering that distance would not be a major problem for expert 'ski-runners' and outdoorsmen such as the four of them were. The problem was that they were carrying almost 700 pounds worth of equipment, including food for a month, radio equipment and weaponry. They decided to leave half the equipment in a safe hiding place to collect after the raid, but they needed to take all their rations as they were under strict orders not to make contact with the local population. Adding to their logistical problems, they were no longer able to head straight across the mountains as their Primus stove had been damaged in the parachute drop. Heat for drying out clothes and for cooking is essential in cold climates, and Grouse realised they would have to stay lower down and head through the Songadalen valley, where they could find supplies of birch wood for making a fire. On 21 October, three days after their arrival, a violent snowstorm burst over the Hardangervidda, severely hampering the four men's efforts to reach the area where they had hoped to set up base. In a matter of hours, autumn was blown away for another year as winter descended with a vengeance.

Such storms make it easy to understand why the Norwegian explorers Amundsen and Nansen trained here before mounting their polar expeditions. Even he got into difficulties. Because it is a plateau with few high peaks, it is easy to forget that the Hardangervidda is over 3,000 feet above sea level and extremely exposed. This is one of the reasons why it has such powerful winds – winds that can whip up very quickly and pose a grave danger even to the most experienced outdoorsman, especially when there is snow. The temperatures can plunge to minus 30 degrees, and together with very high wind-chill factors present conditions as extreme as anywhere on the planet. You can barely see a few feet in front of your nose during a blizzard on the Hardanger, and this brings with it all the obvious dangers of getting lost and succumbing to hypothermia.

The storms can be horrendous. At its angriest, the Hardanger-vidda can kill in a couple of hours. Common sense, initiative and modern equipment can help only so far. Bushcraft, snowcraft or outdoorsmanship – call them what you will – are branches of knowledge, garnered and accumulated down the centuries, passed on from generation to generation by tribes and people throughout the world. To survive in the world's most extreme climates and terrains, you have to *know* how to survive, and knowledge, along with stamina and guts, was what these young Norwegians had in abundance. It is probably fair to say that at this point in history, Norwegians, and Norwegians alone, could have carried out this operation.

Battling against the driving wind, Helberg and Poulsson set off with full packs into a valley known as the Haugedalen, where they knew from their childhood days that there was a hut. To their despair they couldn't find it and were forced to make a heavy march back to the others through the darkness and in a deep fog that had descended on the valley after the wind had as abated almost as quickly as it had arrived. (They later discovered that the hut had been moved to a different location.)

That night they tried to make W/T contact with England, but without success. Communications were a problem in Norway owing to the narrow valleys, steep hills and the often ferocious winter weather. (SOE was eventually able to provide sophisticated sets capable of overcoming the greatest obstacles presented by nature.) Luckily, the party had with them Knut Haugland, one of the best covert signals operators put into the field in occupied territory throughout the entire conflict. For the time being, however, Grouse were unable to get through, and SOE was starting to grow anxious about what might have befallen its advance party. Had intelligence of their imminent arrival leaked out and a German reception committee been sent out to meet them? Perhaps the plane or the parachutes had been spotted or some of them had been badly injured in the parachute drop? They were all genuine fears borne out by the experience of other agents dropped behind enemy lines.

After another night there, the four of them set off on what proved to be, in Poulsson's words 'a heavy and tiresome march', carrying 250 kilos of kit consisting of one wireless, two accumulators, the Eureka homing machine (for contact with aircraft), a hand generator, field equipment, one Sten gun (painted white) plus enough food for thirty days if severely rationed. The equipment was divided up into eight loads of 30 kilos. The four of them would have to make two journeys each every day in order to bring forward all the equipment they needed to their next stopping point.

In their official logbooks and reports, the party would play down the severity of the challenge that faced them in this first week after their arrival, but reading between the lines you quickly understand that it was an extremely punishing journey. The going through the Songadalen valley was very hard; the ice on the lakes had yet to harden; the terrain was rugged and awkward for skiing, and the heavy, wet snow lay deep upon it. If they diverted from their tracks, they sank up to their knees. The violent snowstorm had given way to mild weather and their skis gathered clumps of snow, slowing their progress still further. And although they had brought a small quantity of ski wax with them, they were keen to keep it for the retreat after the raid. 'It was new snow and as the temperature wasn't very low, it kept sticking to our skis,' Helberg recalled.

Nordic skiing, a joy in the right circumstances, has been described as the most complete form of exercise as well as one of the most physically demanding because so many muscles are utilised and great demands are made on the lungs and heart. But if you are exhausted, malnourished, cold and travelling in adverse conditions, it is an extremely stressful pursuit, although still infinitely preferable to the only alternative – that of wading through drifts of snow in boots. Grouse were in an appropriate physical condition to cope with its peculiar demands after their arduous training programmes back in the Cairngorms. Without that conditioning and 'muscle training', they would certainly have struggled even more in the severe conditions they encountered.

Another problem was that they were unable to travel as the crow files, partly because they needed to stay as close as possible to wood supplies. Fire is vital in these conditions. Hot food and drink are essential in extreme cold conditions, but the party also needed to be able to dry out their clothes, which became sodden with melted snow and the sweat generated by their exertions. They wanted to head in as straight a direction as possible, but almost every lake or river they reached was too dangerous to cross as the early winter ice was yet to harden. In the few places where they could cross there was a great deal of surface water on the ice which soaked their feet. According to Poulsson's log, their marches were 'sorrowfully short', and they often advanced only a few kilometres a day. To make matters worse, Poulsson broke a ski stick early on, and it would be a month before he could replace it.

On 24 October, six days after they had landed, the party staggered into an empty farm at a place called Berunuten, exhausted, cold, wet and hungry. Here they found some meat and flour and sat down to their first proper meal since their arrival. It was common practice among those who used the huts on the Hardangervidda to help themselves in an emergency to any supplies they found. Under normal circumstances those who took food would be expected to replace what they could at a later date, or leave some kind of gift or payment. But these were not normal circumstances and Grouse were effectively stealing. 'For the first few days we lived in a tent at the dropping zone but we decided to leave it because it was heavy and we knew there were huts we could break into,' Poulsson recalled. 'At this time of the year, in those conditions, there would be no one else up in the mountains.'

To their delight they also found a toboggan there, and by a remarkable coincidence it turned out to belong to Poulsson. 'It was very strange indeed,' he said. 'I had this toboggan as a boy but it disappeared at the start of the war and of all the coincidences we found it and after that our march became much easier.'

The party went to sleep on full stomachs and, after waking up to fine weather the following morning, it was with greater strength and hope that they continued their trek up the side of the valley towards the huts nearer the Rjukan valley. That day they reached a hut at the top of the Valasjå valley and left their loads there before returning to the Berunuten farm.

Kjelstrup and Poulsson, the strongest of the four, carried a second load up to the hut and spent the night there, while Helberg and Haugland remained in the farm and continued their desperate efforts to make contact with England. Once again they met with no success, and they also failed to appear at the hut on the 27th as arranged after another thick fog had enveloped the valley. They finally made it the following morning, and the four set off once again, having packed as much equipment as possible on to the toboggan. A toboggan is a real benefit if the ground is generally flat and hard and those pulling it can build up a good speed. Once it is gliding along the surface, the toboggan is propelled by its own momentum, thus relieving the pullers of much of the physical stress and allowing them to preserve their energy supplies – something vital in extremely cold conditions, and particularly when nutrition levels fall far below the amounts the body needs to function properly.

The Grouse party had a major scare when, between Valasjådalen and another valley called Bitdalen, they met two men from the nearby town of Rauland who had been out looking for sheep that grazed here during the warmer months. The pair, who were heading towards their hut, knew immediately from the size of their packs and their equipment that these four men were on no ordinary pleasure trip to the mountains. This was Grouse's first encounter with other human life since their arrival over ten days earlier, and it was the scenario they had been warned about during training. They had no choice but to talk to the men. After all, it was not every day on the Hardangervidda at this time of year that you bumped into other people. The four soldiers, their British Army kit hidden from view, bluffed as best they could, hinting that they were on some kind of 'information service', but they made the men promise to keep their mouths shut about meeting them when they returned to Rauland. They seemed to be Jøssings (good Norwegians), but in a country under occupation it was often difficult tell. You never knew who you were talking to – Nazi collaborator, resistance fighter or patriot – and to reveal your allegiance to a stranger could lead to arrest or death.

Telling blatant lies to these men would only have led to confusion, suspicion and rumours back in the local towns. The men asked no more questions. Indeed, they proved very friendly and even went back to their hut to get a hammer and some nails to help fix Poulsson's old toboggan, which had started to crack under the strain of their arduous march.

That evening, when they reached the Bitdalsvatnet lake, the weather deteriorated sharply, and to compound their problems the lake had not yet frozen over and so they were forced to toil along its eastern bank. By the time they reached a hut at Reinar the party were in a pretty poor physical condition. As Poulsson put it: 'We were fairly done in.' Poulsson himself had a throbbing boil on his left hand and his arm was in a sling.

The hard slog on meagre rations had utterly sapped their strength. During the march a day's ration consisted of a quarter of a slab of pemmican (heavily condensed, dried meat mixed with fat and fruits), a handful of groats, four biscuits, a bit of butter, cheese, sugar and chocolate, and one handful of flour. That would barely be enough for a man under ordinary circumstances, let alone in freezing conditions when the body is burning up much more energy to keep warm. When you consider the sheer physical exhaustion they endured wading through the wet snow, the rations were pathetically inadequate.

They decided to split up, with Helberg heading back to the farm at Berunuten to steal as much food as he could carry while Haugland would try once again to make radio contact with the FANYs back at the signals stations in Poundon and Grendon Underwood. Poulsson and Kjelstrup, meanwhile, were to reconnoitre the best way forward for their next march. Their task was made considerably more difficult as Poulsson had left his map behind and had no knowledge of this particular area. The plan was to meet at Reinar three days later.

Helberg experienced horrific conditions on the seven-mile round trip to Berunuten after the temperature plunged and a gale swept across the Hardangervidda from the frozen north-east. Having grown up in its foothills, Helberg and the other Grouse members were well acquainted with the ferocity of winter on Hardangervidda, but they had not expected it to arrive this early or this intensely. When Helberg was finally reunited with the rest of the party, he was at the point of collapse, reduced to an empty wreck by his battle with the strongest forces nature could put his way. In his notes for the official report he was asked to submit at the end of the operation, Poulsson quoted an old Norwegian saying to describe the fortitude that Helberg had shown: 'A man who is a man goes on till he can do no more, and then he goes twice as far.' Later he said of Helberg: 'I am quite a practical man myself, but Helberg was by far the most practical man in the group.'

Poulsson and Kjelstrup fared little better in the dreadful conditions, managing only a few kilometres before returning to Reinar, also at the point of exhaustion. To make matters worse, Poulsson fell through the ice in the river for the second time since they had arrived. There are so many lakes and rivers in the Hardanger that falling into water is a constant hazard. Hypothermia sets in extremely quickly if you fall into water, and you have to get out of your wet clothes and dry yourself within minutes or you will be dead. This can be a major problem if you are travelling by yourself, as the Grouse party often were when they went out hunting or on reconnaissance missions. If they were carrying a spare set of clothes in a rucksack these too would get soaked, so unless they were with a comrade or happened to be near one of the huts that are dotted around some of the lakes they stood very little chance of survival. Pulling yourself out of a frozen lake can be very difficult. The best way to rescue someone is to lie flat on the ice, spreading the body's weight over as great an area as possible, and then use a rope or skis to haul them

out. On this occasion, Kjelstrup was able to help his command-
ing officer to safety.

But there were also some positive developments to emerge
during these gruelling few days, which were pushing them all to
the limit of their very considerable powers of endurance. Firstly,
Poulsson and Kjelstrup found a well-equipped hut, called
Folabu, where they would be able to shelter from the raging
storm and recuperate as best they could before pressing on ('-bu',
incidentally, means 'hut' in Norwegian, and is normally pre-
ceded by the name of the owner). They had also found an ice
bridge over the River Farhovd which they would be able to cross,
thus saving them days of more heavy marching.

Back in Baker Street, meanwhile, the SOE chiefs were beginning to fear the worst for the advance party. The loss of four
good men was a human cost, but there was also the mission to
think about. If they did not hear from Grouse soon they would
have to consider ripping up their plans and launching a new
operation.

Grouse desperately needed a new accumulator, a rechargeable
storage battery, in order to power the W/T set, as the hand generator they were using was not working properly. Poulsson decided
it was imperative to get in touch with Einar Skinnarland's
brother Torstein, the dam-keeper at Møsvatn. After leaving
behind much of their equipment at Reinar and Berunuten, they
transported only their essentials to the Folabu hut.

They also decided that the best base where they could team up
with the British commandos was the Sandvatn hut at Grasfjell.
Although it was five kilometres from the proposed landing place
for the gliders at Skoland, it was set in a remote location, and
they were unlikely to be discovered by the Germans. There were

also few high mountain peaks in the area, making it suitable for efficient wireless communication.

When they finally arrived at the hut, the four were utterly exhausted by their fifteen-day trek through some of the most inhospitable conditions and terrain the northern hemisphere can offer. Under normal conditions for that time of the year, the march would have taken just a fraction of that time. Their resilience is all the more remarkable when you consider the paltry rations they were forced to live off.

'In good weather it would have taken us a couple of days but because the snow was wet, the ground wasn't frozen, the streams and lakes were open [ice-free], it took us one hell of a long time with all that equipment,' recalled Poulsson. 'It was very tiring but because we moved from hut to hut our nights were fairly comfortable. The problem was food. We used up all our rations quickly and became very hungry indeed.'

It was now a matter of urgency that Haugland make radio contact with England. Torstein Skinnarland had supplied them with a new accumulator as well as some food and up-to-date intelligence information about the German forces in the area. As soon as they arrived at the hut, they rigged up some tall antennae masts outside and turned on the W/T set. Once again they had no joy, this time because the set had got wet during the final days of the march and needed to dry out. Three days later, on 9 November, three weeks after they had set off from Scotland, they sent this message, a masterpiece of understatement: 'Happy landing in spite of stones everywhere. Sorry to keep you waiting for message. Snow storm fog forced us to go down valleys. Four feet snow impossible with heavy equipment to cross mountains.'

In a further message three days later Haugland asked for the RAF to drop them more supplies, including forged ration cards for butter and bread, boots, vitamin C tablets and watches (the saboteurs said their standard-issue watches were effectively useless and most of them threw them away after a few days). The violent snowstorm and the physical exertion they had expended trying to operate in it had reminded them that getting enough food – of the right type – was going to be a major priority over the coming weeks. The ration cards would be given to Torstein, who would bring them the supplies, but only so long as it was safe to do so.

The party did their best to recover their strength after their back-breaking march to the hut. Over the following few days, they feasted on a stray sheep and two lambs Haugland had found in a ravine. 'We were very, very hungry at this time so we immediately killed one of the lambs and then skinned it on the floor of the hut,' recalled Haugland.

> We cut up the meat and put it into a big kettle with some dried peas we still had in our emergency rations. It smelled delicious and we all sat down at the table eagerly.
>
> But as one of the group carried the kettle over to us, it dropped on to the floor. We all immediately got down on our hands and knees and even though the floor was very dirty we filled our plates with what we could and ate every last bit. It was delicious. When you are very hungry you will eat anything. The next day we killed the sheep and the other lamb we had tied up. There was a tag around their necks saying the animals belonged to a dentist from southern Norway so we didn't feel guilty. It was a rich man, not a poor farmer we were stealing from.

The man who dropped the stew was the leader, Poulsson, but such was his team's solidarity that his men have always refused to point the finger at him, even years after the event. 'The chaps were not too amused,' Poulsson logged in his official notes.

Once the weather had cleared, the W/T communications were up and running and they were settled in their hut, Grouse were quickly into their operational stride. They had been told that the British troops, whenever they came, would do so by glider, and so they set out on reconnaissance trips in order to find a suitable landing place for them. On 12 November Haugland was able to inform SOE that they had found a site exactly consistent with the guidelines they had been given. The suggested place was five kilometres to the south-west of the Møsvatn dam, and it was flat, free of stones and about 700 yards in length.

Haugland was also able to inform London that, according to Skinnarland's sources, Dr Brun, the manager of the hydroelectric plant, had fled Vemork with his wife and was thought to have escaped to Sweden. This gave SOE time to prepare a reception committee so that they would waste no time in interrogating him and putting the final details of the operation together.

Haugland's messages had to be short – and the more quickly transmitted the better – so as to avoid interception by the Germans. Reading the telegrams today (the originals can be found at the Public Record Office in Kew, and copies of some of them at the Norwegian Resistance Museum in Oslo), you quickly become aware that Haugland was a master of his art. All his messages, decoded back in England, are short, accurate and densely informative – not a word out of place, not a word wasted.

Haugland is a very interesting character, who does not

comfortably fit the image of the SOE-trained saboteur with a lantern jaw and knowledge of a hundred different ways of killing a man up a dimly lit alley. There was no question that he could carry out any of the dark tasks SOE demanded of its 'students', but he was also a highly cerebral character, as were so many of the W/T operators during the war. The role of these operators has been overshadowed by the more colourful and overtly heroic actions of the saboteurs, but it was of the very greatest importance to the war effort. It is fair to say that without them there would have been no meaningful resistance movements. A man of exceptionally strong convictions and fastidious over the smallest details, Haugland was one of the very best in the business, some even said *the* best.

Covert communication with London was virtually the only means of contact between the occupied countries and the Allies. Messages were smuggled out by other means, but from an operational point of view, in terms of troop or ship movements and so on, information had to be relayed with great haste. The W/T operators working in conjunction with their intelligence contacts were the eyes, ears and mouth of the Allies in occupied Europe. The Germans readily understood the threat posed by the W/T operators and had developed highly sophisticated detection techniques to capture them, capable of pinpointing the location of a transmitting station within minutes. They were able to intercept all the messages arriving and being sent out at the SOE stations in Poundon and Grendon Underwood and other Allied signals stations virtually at their leisure – the problem was cracking the codes.

Until they succeeded in this, their best hope of disrupting the communications traffic was to capture the operators in their occupied territory. W/T operators behind enemy lines led a highly dangerous existence, constantly having to move their heavy equipment from one location to the next, to avoid detection. The weight and size of the transmitters were a major problem. At the beginning of SOE operations, a transmitter/receiver set weighed up to 30 pounds, although this was later reduced to 14. Power was also a major headache owing to the security precautions they were forced to take, and in Grouse's case because of the remoteness of their location, where electricity was not available. Charging batteries could be the biggest problem for those in the field. In the end the hand generator was the best solution, but it proved to be far from perfect.

They also had to transmit vital information in complicated codes as quickly as possible. The longer they were on air, the more chance the Germans had of capturing them. This was less of a problem for Haugland and Skinnarland, who were to some extent protected by the wilderness of the Hardangervidda, but on a number of occasions they too had to quickly pack up their equipment and flee after hearing the sound of a German search plane overhead.

Back in London, on 15 November SOE and Combined Operations held a meeting at SOE's Norwegian headquarters at Chiltern Court, Baker Street. Around the table on this occasion were Lieutenant Colonel Henneker and Lieutenant Commander Wedlake, both of Combined Operations, and Lieutenant Colonel Wilson, Professor Tronstad and Majors Rheams and Nicholls of SOE. It was decided that two members of the Grouse party would guide the British troops to the plant in two separate groups. The other two would remain with the W/T equipment and destroy the

Eureka machine as soon as the gliders had landed. The operation was to be called Freshman, and it would be launched in what they called the 'moon period' starting in three days' time. (The moon period was the time either side of the full moon when there would be the most light.) Less than a week after completing their gruelling march across the Hardanger, Grouse were put on stand-by to prepare for the gliders' arrival.

At the meeting Tronstad put forward new proposals for the destruction of the plant, saying that General Hansteen of the Norwegian Army had expressed strong anxieties about causing widespread damage to the plant, fearing that it would be put out of action entirely for years to come. About two hundred locals depended on the plant for their livelihood, and the fertilisers they produced there were of immense importance to the national economy. The Norsk Hyrdo station, designed to manufacture various commercial and industrial products, was Norway's largest industrial enterprise, and to destroy it completely would be a major blow to the country.

When pressed, Tronstad, said he thought a successful demolition job would put the 'heavy water' part of the plant out of action for between one and a half to two years. Such a scenario would give the Allies an almost unassailable lead in the race to build the A-bomb.

Tronstad's information was crucial to the planning of the operation. He knew every inch of the plant's layout and details of the heavy water apparatus as well as the working practices and shift times of the staff there. A subsequent official report in which Tronstad was recommended for an award stated: 'His technical advice was of the greatest value since it proved that the operation could be effectively carried out by a small party without danger to the lives of loyal Norwegians and the causing of damage which would involve Norway in grave economic loss after the conclusion of the war.' Even fresher intelligence was provided by Dr Brun, the chief manager at Vemork, who had just recently arrived in England after he and his wife had been smuggled out of Norway by the resistance.

During the waiting period, Grouse were given major cause for alarm when two men came to the hut on separate occasions. SOE's instructions were to kill anyone who discovered them unless they could be sure they were patriots. These two, it turned out, were good Norwegians. The first was a man from Oslo who saw the antennnae masts and came to investigate. They explained vaguely that they were providing an 'information service' listening to the wireless, but it quickly transpired that the man was a patriot. The second man was called Brorusten, and both Poulsson and Haugland knew him from before the war. He asked no questions.

The risk of visits by strangers was a source of great anxiety for the party. Under no circumstances could they afford to have their cover blown, but equally they did not want to have to kill any of their compatriots unless they knew for certain that they were quislings. To kill an innocent man just because he *might* spread gossip was repugnant to them, but this was wartime and the rules were different.

Despite the remoteness of the party's location, the visits of the two men highlighted Grouse's vulnerability. It was a strange sensation for them: three of them were locals who had grown up in the mountains and the fourth knew the area well, but now they felt like strangers in their own land, professional bandits in the wild, dedicated to the overthrow of an alien force. Many of their friends and families were living just a few kilometres away, unaware that their loved ones were camped up on the plateau, putting their own lives in serious danger as well as those of the locals, who would suffer lethal reprisals from the Nazis if it was discovered they had been in contact with the young British-trained saboteurs.

The party had no choice but to live in the mountains. Had they tried to operate from Rjukan or one of the villages, they would have been flushed out in an instant. There were not just Germans in their midst but quislings too, and in small communities any remotely suspicious behaviour could lead to immediate danger.

During the stand-by period Haugland began supplying daily weather reports and accurate intelligence information. Thanks largely to Torstein Skinnarland, but also to their own reconnaissance sorties, Grouse were able to inform London about German strengths in the area. There were, they discovered, now twelve men at the Møsvatn dam in a hotel, twelve at the Vemork plant and forty down the road at Rjukan. All the troops were under the command of an elderly captain based in Rjukan. Most of the officers and men were Austrians, a handful of whom were invalids wounded earlier in the war, and not 'fighting fit'. Periodically, groups of first-class German 'shock troops' would arrive in the town and stay for a week before moving on. There were almost 300,000 German troops in Norway at this time, and reinforcements could be quickly deployed in the event of an attack.

Skinnarland also reported to Grouse that some German civilians had recently arrived in Rjukan and were thought to be Gestapo, as they appeared to have little to do with the Vemork plant and were unlikely to be scientists. At the end of September a group of about twenty 'sappers' had visited Vemork to lay mines around the site. Every day high-ranking German officers visited the plant to discuss ways of improving its security.

At the beginning of October General von Falkenhorst, the commander-in-chief of the German Army in Norway, visited the plant with the German consul from Oslo. The general made a long speech to the plant's directors and managers and to the guards, warning them that a number of British commando raids in Norway in recent months had led him to believe that Vemork was vulnerable to a similar attack. According to Skinnarland's sources at the plant, he mentioned his great admiration for British commandos and personally demonstrated their tactics when attacking guards. He told the assembly that the commandos would be equipped with automatic weapons and silencers, chloroform, hand grenades and knuckle-dusters. He said he believed that, if they came, the British would be disguised as civilians and would arrive by bus or train with plain clothes over their uniforms.

Tellingly, he also admitted that he did not have the resources to place a suitable garrison at the plant (he said a hundred soldiers would be required to be absolutely safe) and that he was pressing ahead with plans to lay dozens of mines. The Germans' reinforcement of the plant's defences was focused on the giant penstocks (water pipes) to the rear of the installation, in the belief that its position in the steep gorge made it impregnable to attack from the front.

The Germans also erected searchlights on the roof of the plant, a machine-gun post was hidden in a hut near the entrance, and a network of booby traps and tripwires was installed. Again, most of these were concentrated to the rear of the plant where it was feared an attack might come.

The bridge over the valley from the road to the plant was closed off by a gate at the road end and was patrolled by two guards, who spent much of their time in the sentry hut playing cards and keeping warm. Situated about 150 miles inland, Rjukan was a sleepy town far from any active theatre of war, and the idea of British troops even being able to reach the area was fanciful to those garrisoned there.

Working on these intelligence updates together with Tronstad's suggestions and diagrams of the plant, the operation's organisers decided that the best way for the attackers to proceed would be to liquidate the guards on the bridge using silenced weapons before scrambling up a steep slope to the railway line that fed the plant. One of the guards would be a German armed with a carbine rifle and the other a Norwegian, recognisable by his shiny cap and brown coat and armed only with a revolver. All telephone lines leading along the road and from the plant were to be cut before the advance.

The attackers would then cut through the fence and enter the factory yard between the powerhouse and the electrolysis plant before attempting to force an entry into the basement of the Hydro plant, where the heavy water was kept. Inside the commandos would find four engineers, all of them known to be 'true' Norwegians who were not to be harmed in any circumstances.

Over eight months had passed since news of the increased production of heavy water at Vemork had reached Whitehall. There had been countless meetings and communiqués between the parties involved, as well as disputes about the nature of the operation. With every day that passed Hitler's scientists had moved steadily closer to realising their ambition of building the first weapon in history that could destroy an entire city. But the waiting was now over as thirty-four British commandos packed their bags, left their training stations and were transported amid the tightest security to the north of Scotland.

4

Gliding to Disaster

By the end of September 1942, details of different plans of attack had been drawn up only in outline by Combined Operations. The memos passing between the various interested parties at this time make it clear that all options were still on the table. There were, however, good reasons why the planners struggled to produce a master scheme for the operation. Whichever way they looked at it, they could conclude that there was only a slender of chances of getting their men out safely.

One of the plans under consideration was to drop a group of about thirty commandos by Catalina flying boat on Møsvatn lake, from where the groups would retreat to the mountains for the night and then launch an attack within twenty-four hours, before they were discovered. The group would split into three sub-parties and meet at a prearranged rendezvous. All three would attack the plant at once after overcoming any resistance. One would blow up the heavy water itself, the second would destroy its capacity to restart production by blowing up the apparatus used to create the heavy water, while the third would blow up and block the road leading to the plant in both directions to stall the arrival of German reinforcements.

The three parties would then withdraw back to Møsvatn,

about 10 kilometres to the west, where they would be picked up
by flying boat for their return to the UK. There were a number of
obvious problems with this plan. First, flying boats need water
to land on, and Norway's lakes started to ice over by the end of
October. Second, the giant aircraft ran a high risk of being spotted by one of the guards at the Møsvatn dam. Third, the escape
was fraught with risk as the alarm would quickly be raised, and
even if the soldiers could get back to Møsvatn lake and board the
flying boat the slow, lumbering aircraft would present an easy
target for interceptor fighters on its return home.

The indecision of Combined Operations had started to irritate the highest authorities in Whitehall as well as SOE, whose
advance party, Grouse, had been twiddling its thumbs in various
stately homes and holding houses dotted around Britain. In
early October the Lord President of the Council sent his private
secretary to Combined Operations headquarters in Richmond
Terrace, tucked between Whitehall and the Thames Embank-
ment and a short walk from Parliament Square, to inject some
urgency into the proceedings.

The scribbled notes and diagrams made by an officer from
Combined Operations at a meeting on 13 October show that not
until then was a concrete strategy laid down. A sketch pinpoints
the landing area for the gliders near the Møsvatn dam while a
note spells out the line of attack.

> Lorry with our men could drive up [to Vemork entrance on
> suspension bridge] and 'do in' sentry . . . party attacks con-
> tainers which should explode and wreck whole installation
> . . . 2hr delay should be used so as to warn families to fly . . .
> attacking party should come from north side to cross bridge

... access is barred on south side by impossible precipices
... Skinnarland and wife would have to be warned to visit
step-parents in Rjukan ... lorry bus strongly recommended
... nearest garrisons 120 kilo away ... Rjukan has a few
Jerrys ...

(There were, in fact, forty 'Jerrys' there.)

The hastily scrawled notes also make mention of 'killing
whole valley' and taking precautions to turn off some taps. What
was meant by this is not clear, but it gives an insight into the confusion about what exactly they were going to attack and what
measures they were going to take to avoid causing harm to the
locals.

Within days of the meeting the plans for the operation were
finally approved. It was to be called Operation Freshman, and
the explicit objective of the mission was: 'To destroy the stocks
of Lurgan [code name for heavy water], the importance of which
far transcends all other objectives, and only after their destruction has been assured to carry out such demolitions as will
deny to the enemy the productive capacity of the Norsk Hydro
Works'.

The attack would be a glider-borne operation, the first
attempted by Allies in the Second World War. The attacking
party would consist of about thirty-six Royal Engineers of the
1st Airborne Division, including three officers, plus the four
members of the advance group and the four-man crew of the two
gliders. They were to fight their way to the target if need be, and
anyone wounded was to be given morphine and left behind.
After carrying out the raid, the British commandos were to
escape on foot to Sweden, fighting their way over 400 kilometres

to the frontier if necessary. Grouse were to disappear into their mountain retreat and lie low until the German searches of the area were over.

None of the British soldiers would be given any details about the operation, or even told what country they were going to, until a few days before they were due to leave. They were told only that they had been hand-chosen to carry out a raid deep behind enemy lines. They were warned about the great dangers involved and offered the opportunity to withdraw if they had compelling personal reasons, such as a young family or a pregnant wife. Those who pulled out would return to their regular unit with no questions asked.

The operation was cloaked in the greatest secrecy and an imaginative cover story was created to explain why they were leaving their regular units and undergoing special training. The story, the brainchild of a Lieutenant Colonel Henneker, of the Royal Engineers Airborne Division, seconded to Combined Operations, was that they were to undergo an endurance trial in a competition with their US equivalents in various parts of the country with the winners receiving a trophy called the Washington Cup. The gliders to be used for the operation, meanwhile, were housed in hangars so that German reconnaissance and photographic aircraft could not see them.

The soldiers were put through an intensive and punishing commando training programme involving a series of marches with full equipment (80 pounds per man). The idea was not just to toughen them up, but also to expose any who might not be up to the task. After the basic training, the men were taken to Snowdonia on 27 October and split into pairs. They were then dropped 'blind' somewhere on a mountain and told to live rough for four nights, using a map and compass to guide them to a pre-arranged rendezvous. They were given the type of rations they would have in Norway in order for their bodies to adapt before departure. Some of the men were withdrawn after the Wales trip, but the rest were then given courses in high-impact explosives, first at the SOE station at Hertford North and then at Port Sunlight in the Wirral and Fort William in the Highlands. The commandos were never told where they were and were taken to and from the training camps under cover of darkness.

They carried out mock raids so that the men were able to enter the room in total darkness, feel their way around the apparatus and lay the explosives as if they were blind.

Like SOE recruits, they were also instructed in the arts of 'irregular warfare', such as silent killing, street fighting, using the commando dagger and the garrotte, and killing with their bare hands. A mock-up village with pop-up soldiers was used to train the men in street fighting and how to draw their weapons like a Wild West outlaw.

At the end of October a Combined Operations meeting was called to discuss the plans for the escape after the raid. Lieutenant Colonel Henneker opened the discussion by saying he considered it would be 'more soldierly' if the raiders were to fight their way out in one body. Major de Bruyne of MI9, the wartime secret service agency specialising in escape and evasion, pointed out that their chances of survival in a running fight over a distance of between 200 and 400 miles in hostile terrain would be very slim. He proposed that the group split into pairs and take different routes to the Swedish border, disguising themselves as Norwegians. Henneker conceded the point, but said that 'as far as possible two stupid men should not be paired together'.

MI9 were detailed to produce a plan for the escape with at least three different routes. They were also to provide thirty-five 'escape sets', thirty-five purses containing 200 Norwegian kroner, maps made from silk (1:100,000 scale) and a brief to explain how the party could disguise themselves as locals in terms of clothes and habits of behaviour. The troops would begin their escape in battledress, but as soon as possible they were to change into civilian clothes, tailored by MI9 to look as authentically Norwegian as possible. The clothes were to be issued to the soldiers at the earliest possible opportunity so that they would be well worn by the start of the operation. They were told they must use their shaving kits every day of the escape. Soldiers who sported moustaches had to shave them off as Norwegian men did not wear them. They were told to grow their hair long, Norwegian-style, so as not to arouse suspicion. 'No hair oil to be used before the operation' was one further stipulation, presumably because it could not be obtained within Norway itself. They were also instructed to leave a few kroner in any boat they might have to steal as a 'thank you' to the owner. If captured, they were to give only their name, rank and number as the Geneva Convention required them to do.

The meeting also stressed the importance of full British battledress being worn during the attack itself so the Germans could have no doubt that this was an Allied military operation and not the work of locals, thereby preventing risk of reprisals.

Each soldier's equipment included the following: normal battledress with civilian clothes underneath, a white wind-proof anorak, a seaman's woollen sweater, a pair of blue ski trousers, an army shirt, boots and gaiters, one pair of Norwegian-pattern shoes, six pairs of socks, string vests and long pants, khaki mittens, gloves with trigger finger, one pair of rubber gloves (for explosives), cap, balaclava, skiing scarf and steel helmet.

Other equipment included a light waterproof sleeping bag weighing about four pounds, a Bergen rucksack, an alcohol compass, a Sten gun with magazines, ten days of rations, a first-aid kit and explosive charges.

Major Munthe, a Gordon Highlander attached to SOE (and the son of Swedish author Axel Munthe), compiled a memo with a few phrases he thought might be handy for the British troops during their escape: '*Jeg har vert ut og kopt lit proviant til Mor.*' (I have just been out buying some stores for mother.) '*Unskyld men jag maa hurtigst til tannlegeren.*' (Sorry, but I must get to the dentist as quickly as possible – Munthe suggests that this one should be spoken with a stone or a cork in the mouth. '*Leve Norge og Heil Quisling!*' (Long Live Norway and Hail Quisling!)

There is something mildly comic, almost Monty Python-esque, about this, but it shows the lengths SOE went to, even for hastily arranged operations like Freshman, to ensure the efficiency of the plan and the security of their personnel. Munthe's suggestions were perfectly sensible because it was highly unlikely that any Germans they might encounter would speak Norwegian.

Hollywood films, not least *The Heroes of Telemark*, have succeeded in creating an impression among many that specialist British organisations like SOE and Combined Operations were a small club of gung-ho adventurers run by daring, madcap public school boys. But the truth was that SOE, for all the criticism it received in the early years, was by now a highly professional and efficient body, run by battle-hardened and intelligent soldiers. What they lacked in resources, they made up for in ingenuity and lateral thought. (While we are on the subject of myths and nonsense, the 1963 Kirk Douglas picture about the Vemork raid was roundly condemned as utter rubbish by the real saboteurs, some of whom had helped in the making of the picture. Even today, the very mention of the film to the survivors provokes a burst of invective and stick-waving.)

In the middle of November, just before the start of the November moon period, the party travelled north, close to the Skitten aerodrome near Wick in the flat, treeless landscape of Caithness on the north-east coast of Scotland. It was from here that the operation would be launched.

Haugland sent information on 15 November to the effect that the snow lay 30 centimetres deep at the landing place and that it had frozen hard. He said the march to the plant should take no more than five hours if the weather held. On the 18th Louis Mountbatten, the Chief of Combined Operations, sent the following memorandum to the Prime Minister via Downing Street's scientific adviser, Lord Cherwell:

> Thirty-six [there were actually thirty-four] all ranks of the Airborne Division will be flown in towed gliders to destroy the Power Station, electrical plant and stocks of 'heavy water' at Vemork on any night between 19/20 November and 26/27 November. The Germans have about 1¼ tons of 'heavy water', of which nearly all is stored at Vemork. When they have five tons they will be able to start production of a new form of explosive a thousand times more potent than any in use to-day. If the operation is successful, it will be

three years before the Germans can accumulate five tons of 'heavy water.' If it fails, they will get the stock in 18 months. The raiders hope to escape through Sweden.

Churchill replied: 'C.C.O. approved. Ask Lord Cherwell to report to me on the technical aspect. He is already my adviser on the main question. Signed: W.S.C.'

Of all countries in Europe, Norway was probably the least suitable for glider operations, which were extremely hazardous ventures even in the best of terrains and weather conditions. Troops preferred parachute operations, even though they too were relatively unsophisticated and dangerous by modern-day standards. Glider operations need flat landing places, and these were virtually impossible to find in Norway with its steep, craggy, twisting valleys and fjords. Landing on frozen lakes was out of the question as the weight of a glider packed with dozens of soldiers and their equipment would shatter the surface or create its own wall of rock-hard ice as it slid. Furthermore, the broken terrain also generated powerful wind pockets that could toss the unwieldy gliders around like gossamer.

To make matters worse, Norway was experiencing dreadful weather that autumn, and with no accurate meteorological forecasting at that time there was a great risk that the party could set off in fine conditions only to be struck suddenly by powerful winds, particularly over the Hardangervidda. Glider pilots had one of the most dangerous jobs in the Allied war effort, and their chances of survival over a long period of operations were slim.

After they were put on stand-by for the imminent arrival of Freshman, the four members of Grouse went over the plan time

and again so as to avoid any cock-ups on the night. Their efficiency would be crucial to the entire operation. Helberg and
Poulsson were to put up the landing lights and the Eureka
homing machine at the designated place to guide the gliders on
to the marshlands near Møsvatn dam.

Haugland and Kjelstrup were to wait by the wireless for messages from London before proceeding to the landing place. The
following night, Helberg was to cut the telephone lines before
joining Poulsson in leading the British saboteurs to Vemork.
Haugland and Kjelstrup were detailed to destroy the Eureka set
and collect the landing lights before returning to the hut. The
two pairs had planned to go their separate ways and lie low for
a week after the raid before meeting at a hut near the dam. On
the night of 18 November they sat in the hut nervously awaiting
a message from London, but were disappointed when the code
word 'Boy' crackled through the set, indicating that the operation would not take place that night.

At a quarter past five the following evening, Haugland
reported that the weather was good over Telemark. There was a
moderate wind from the west, a bit of patchy cloud and visibility
of 10 kilometres. Shortly afterwards the code sign 'Girl' crackled through his receiver. The operation was on.

The thirty-four Royal Engineers, in full battledress and heavily laden with equipment, made their way across the runway at
Skitten aerodrome to two Horsa gliders attached to Halifax
bombers. There would be seventeen commandos in each glider,
plus two RAF crew who could communicate with the crew of the
Halifax by wires running through the towing rope (among the
glider pilots were two Australians). The planners had figured
that about fifteen men were needed to carry out the operation,

but they doubled the number and split them into two gliders because if one crashed or was wiped out in a gun battle after landing the other contingent might still be able to carry out the attack.

When the four aircraft took off at around six o'clock the weather was fair and mild. There was, though, a light breeze, and one of the meteorological experts at the base warned against launching the operation. The wind began to pick up as they crossed the North Sea. The gliders began to bobble and shake and the stomachs of those on board began to tighten. An operation of this nature would always provoke powerful sensations of trepidation and exhilaration in equal measure, and sitting in a wooden, engineless aircraft being buffeted by the wind would have done little to calm their nerves.

Helberg and Poulsson set up the Eureka machine, which was to alert them of the planes' imminent arrival. This homing device had been developed at the start of the war, and although it was fairly unsophisticated compared to the highly accurate systems of today, it was invaluable to SOE operatives, whose work depended greatly on communication with the RAF. The aircraft was fitted with a machine known as Rebecca, which sent out a pulse to the Eureka on the ground, which in turn automatically replied on a different frequency and informed the crew of its location.

Haugland, the machine's operator that night, put on the earphones and turned on the power. When the approaching planes picked up the signal from Eureka, Haugland would hear a distinctive hum that would tell him they were close by. They laid out the landing lights, three red ones in a triangle each 100 yards apart with a fourth flashing white light in the apex, which was to point

The two most powerful Germans in Norway during the war:
Reichskommissar Josef Terboven (*far right, pointing*) and Generaloberst
Nikolaus von Falkenhorst (*third right, in white coat*).

18th November, 1942.

Memorandum for the Prime Minister.

Operation "FRESHMAN".

Thirty-six all ranks of the Airborne Division will be flown in towed Gliders to destroy the Power Station, electrical plant and stocks of "heavy water" at Vemork in Norway on any night between 19/20th November and 26/27th November.

The Germans have about 1½ tons of "heavy water", of which nearly all is stored at Vemork. When they have 5 tons they will be able to start production of a new form of explosive a thousand times more potent than any in use to-day.

If the operation is successful, it will be three years before the Germans can accumulate 5 tons of "heavy water". If it fails, they will get the stock in 18 months. The raiders hope to escape through Sweden.

Louis Mountbatten

Chief of Combined Operations.

The memo from Mountbatten to Churchill sent the day before Operation Freshman was launched.

The target, the 'hydro-electric plant' at Vemork.

LOCAL NR. 62/SRL 866.
CIPHER MESSAGE FROM SWAN.

DESP. 1424 11.12.42.
RECD. 1640 11.12.42.

TRANSLATION.

GEORGE SK.

GLIDER PLANE FELL DOWN AT HELLELAND CHURCH STOP.

FIVE MEN STOP.

TWO KILLED CERTAINLY SOME WOUNDED STOP.

ALL TAKEN PRISONER INTERROGATED FOR TWO HOURS STOP.

ALL GAVE RJUKAN POWER STATION AS TARGET STOP.

THEY WERE ALL SUBSEQUENTLY SHOT.

GEORGE.

58° 31' 6" N.
6° 7' 25" E

An SOE agent sent news about the fate of Operation Freshman but it was years before the full truth was established.

Wreckage of one of the gliders used in Operation Freshman.

Lieutenant Colonel Jack Wilson, head of SOE's Norwegian section.

2nd Lieutenant Jens Poulsson, the leader of the Operation Grouse/Swallow.

2nd Lieutenant Knut Haugland

Sergeant Claus Helberg

Sergeant Arne Kjelstrup

Einar Skinnarland

2nd Lieutenant Joachim
Rønneberg, head of
Gunnerside.

2nd Lieutenant Knut
Haukelid

2nd Lieutenant Kaspar
Idland

Sergeant Frederik Kayser

Sergeant Birger
Strømsheim

Sergeant Hans Storhaug

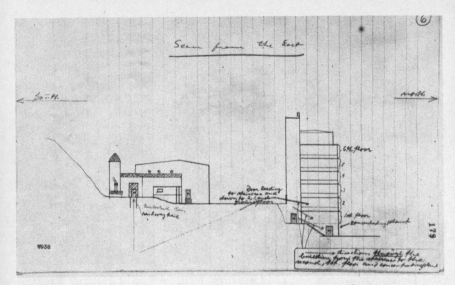

The saboteurs were fortunate in having accurate information from Norwegians who had worked at the plant. This sketch shows how they were to enter the basement where the heavy water was stored. In the event they were forced to crawl through a narrow cable duct.

The town of Rjukan, as seen from the neighbouring mountainside.

Allied intelligence aerial
photographs of the
plant and the
surrounding area,
(*above*) and details
provided by Leif
Tronstad and Dr Jonar
Brun (*right*), helped the
planners to brief the
saboteurs.

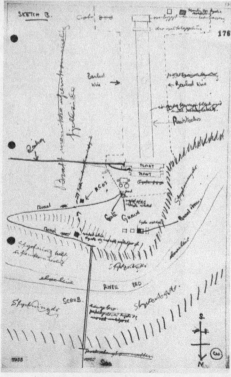

...night there came the first detailed story of Allied wreckers being landed by plane in ...itory, completing their sabotage at a German controlled war factory, and leaving for ...his daring enterprise, by three Norwegian patriots, so enraged the Germans that they shot 17 hostages, most of whom had been in gaol for some time.

s Came–and Left–by Air:
Nazi Works Wrecked

THE Norsk Hydro works, which were the target of airborne wreckers on Saturday night, is a subsidiary of the famous I. G. Farben chemical factory. The plant produces sulphur and nitrogen for high explosives for Germany. It is 80 miles from Oslo.

PLANE LANDED ON LAKE

From **RALPH HEWINS,** Daily Mail Correspondent

STOCKHOLM, Monday.

THREE Norwegian patriots in British uniforms were landed from a plane on a frozen lake, 80 miles northwest of Oslo, during the half-moonlight of Saturday night.

The men, skilled saboteurs, succeeded in blowing up part of the great German-controlled Norsk Hydro Electric plant at Rjukan.

Then the patriots returned to the ice-covered lake, clambered aboard. The engines revved, and the journey back to Britain was begun.

That I was told to-day by a person in a position to know, is the story behind the sudden execution yesterday of 17 Norwegians on the usual charges of "Communism, sabotage, and helping the enemy."

Spite at being outwitted led the German S.S. and Rediess, Norway's chief of police, to murder those 17 hostages.

The attack on the factory, producing quantities of nitrates and fertilisers, is one of the most sensational pieces of sabotage since the Commando raids on Lofoten and St. Nazaire.

At least one section of the plant is known to have been totally destroyed, and the explosions as the factory blew up were heard for many miles.

The factory is in West Fjord Valley, 3,000ft. above sea-level, in Telemark province, which gives its name to a most spectacular ski run.

Knew Country

It is the largest in the world and employs between 10,000 and 12,000 people. When the Germans occupied Norway it was taken over by the Reich I. G. Farben Combine.

The explosions were timed so that only German and Quisling night-watchmen were killed.

In case the men were dropped by parachute and received signals from resident patriots, the Germans are maintaining a widespread search for internal conspirators.

Norwegian circles in Stockholm believe this is a build-up for further executions and reprisals.

The saboteurs, however, knew the ground intimately, as it is some of the most famous ski-ing country in Scandinavia. They had no need of help from local agents.

Best known of the 17 who have been executed was Ottar Lie, secretary of the Norwegian Communist Party since 1927. He had been in a concentration camp for the past three months.

The *Daily Mail* carried news of the attack, although the details were incorrect.

downwind. The white light was to flash the letter L for London and was to be continuously directed at the aircraft.

The party sat anxiously listening for the drone of the two Halifax bombers towing the gliders. They waited and waited until, at twenty to ten, Helberg and Poulsson heard the sound of an aircraft to the south-west and Haugland could make out a dim signal from the Eureka machine. At last, the British were here! Within hours they would be advancing on the Vemork plant and their first direct confrontation with the occupying forces. Their spirits leapt at the sound, but when the plane was no more than about two kilometres away, a meagre distance in the vast expanse of the Hardangervidda, they heard it turn away. Their hearts sank.

Over the next two hours they thought they could hear the occasional drone of a plane as the RAF crews scoured the white wilderness below for their designated dropping point. (It was difficult to tell whether it was one or both of the planes they heard.) The cloud was starting to thicken and, confused by the bewildering array of lakes and ravines below them, the crew could not be certain they had found the landing site. The Grouse party felt helpless. At 2300 hours they heard the plane for the last time, and half an hour later Helberg and Poulsson returned to the hut.

'We definitely heard the noise of aircraft engines, but nothing happened,' Helberg later recalled. 'The weather wasn't too bad. There was some cloud cover and some wind, but it certainly wasn't a storm or anything like that. The moon was out and it wasn't very dark.'

After the war Haugland also confirmed that there had been some contact via the Eureka/Rebecca system and that they had heard aircraft above. 'I tried to make contact with England to warn them about the weather, but it wasn't possible to get through. I heard interference on my [Eureka] headphones and soon afterwards we heard the noise of the engines but it just went away.'

At five to midnight Combined Operations HQ received a vague message that one of the gliders had been released over the sea close to the Norwegian coast, but there was no news of the aircraft towing it. At 0330 hours they received another telling them that one of the Halifaxes had landed safely at Wick. Ten search planes were scrambled at first light to search the coastline for the downed glider but they returned having found nothing.

Over the coming days there was great confusion about the fate of the two gliders and the other aircraft. The following day intelligence sources intercepted a German communiqué, stating that two gliders and one plane were forced down and that the 'sabotage' troops were 'engaged and annihilated'. What really happened to those soldiers would not become entirely clear until British troops returned to Norway at the very end of the war.

One of the Halifaxes, with its glider in tow, had reached the drop zone but, unsure of their exact location and running low on fuel, the crew had decided to turn for home. Struggling for altitude, the plane found itself in thick cloud and heavy turbulence. The tow-rope froze solid and then snapped, sending the glider on a terrifying spiral to the earth, crashing nose first at over 100 mph. The planes were near the Norwegian coast when the break occurred, which would explain the message from the RAF crew to HQ that the glider had been released over the sea. In fact the glider crashed high in the freezing mountains at a place called Fyljesdal near Lysefjord, killing seven on board on impact. Another had a spinal injury and was paralysed from the hips down, one had two broken legs, one a broken jaw and one a broken skull and severe breathing problems.

Tom Conacher, the RAF warrant officer on the Halifax, said: 'We turned around and set course for home. We were practically at the coast when it began to ice up very badly. I noticed that the rope [attached to the glider] was beginning to ice up too and the glider started getting out of line. Then it just snapped and I saw it peeling away. There was a terrific orange flash away to our port that I took to be an aircraft.'

The five uninjured commandos from the glider tended the wounded as best they could before three of them set out to get help. The five could have tried to escape to Sweden, but they didn't want to desert their comrades. They gave themselves up to the authorities in the expectation that their colleagues, in accordance with the Geneva Convention, would be given medical treatment and they would all be sent to a POW camp until the end of the war.

When a group of Norwegians returned with the men to the crash site, a vision from hell greeted them. They saw eight corpses, including that of one soldier who had crawled clear of the aircraft only to die of exposure and loss of blood. Another's stomach was ripped open and was frozen to the ground by his intestines. The injured were given morphine and carried on makeshift stretchers down the hillside to a nearby farm. Shortly afterwards, two groups of Germans arrived, one party of regular Wehrmacht soldiers and another of SS troops under the command of a Gestapo officer.

The dead men were unceremoniously dumped in shallow graves and the Germans refused Norwegian requests over the following days to give them a proper burial. Later, locals stole up to the graves and erected a fence around them to stop animals getting to them. After the war the bodies were exhumed and given a proper ceremony at Eiganes churchyard near Stavanger.

The five uninjured men were held until January in Grini concentration camp near Oslo, and, bound and blindfolded, they were then taken to Trandum Wood and shot in the head. After the war they were reburied in the Commonwealth War Graves plot at Vestre Gravlund on the outskirts of the Norwegian capital.

The four injured British troops were Corporal James Cairncross of Hawick, Driver Peter Farrell of Marylebone, Lance Corporal Trevor Masters of Cobh, County Cork, and Sapper Eric Smith of Paddington. They were taken away by the Gestapo, and what happened to them makes for especially gruesome reading. Allied investigations into their deaths led to a war crimes trial in which all the grisly details of their torture and death were laid out to a horrified tribunal. Even by the brutal standards of the Gestapo, the treatment of the four badly injured young soldiers was grotesque in the extreme. After the five uninjured Royal Engineers had been taken to Grini, the remaining four were left in 'Prison A', at a street called Lagårdsveien, and dealt with by the Gestapo. The men were already in great agony and distress from the wounds suffered in the crash, and had not been treated since the Germans had taken them away.

Three of them were beaten and half strangled with leather straps before their torturers stood on their chests and throats and injected air into their bloodstreams. They died slowly and in extreme pain. The fourth man, the least badly injured, was in a separate cell from the others and could hear the terrifying screams, wails and groans followed by the deathly silence of his comrades. He lay there for a night awaiting his turn, but he was 'spared' the horror of a long-drawn-out, humiliating death and was shot in the back of the head as he descended the stairs into a basement the following day. The bodies of all four men were taken out to sea and dumped overboard. At the end of hostilities three men were charged with murdering the young soldiers by the War Crimes Commission. Two were sentenced to death and the third was given life imprisonment for his lesser role.

There was also a great deal of confusion about the fate of the other Halifax and its glider, but when their fate was finally established the details were equally shocking. On 11 December, three weeks after Operation Freshman had been launched, SOE received a message from one of its agents operating in the south of Telemark, working under the code name Swan. He said the glider plane had crashed in the mountains near a church at Helleland, close to a town called Egersund, about 200 kilometres from the intended dropping zone. Two or three soldiers were killed instantly and several were wounded. 'All taken prisoner interrogated for two hours,' it continued. 'They were all subsequently shot.'

The picture became clearer following information received from another SOE operative, code-named Crow, and a resistance fighter called Arne Lima, who worked for the local branch of the Norwegian Labour Service and was the first to reach the crash site. Crow, who had been captured by the Gestapo, was taken to the prison where the survivors were held to act as interpreter. He said that two or three of the group had died in the crash and that another four or five had been badly injured. One had a spinal injury and was paralysed from the hips down. He was lying on the floor of the prison with a blanket over him. Another, with a broken leg and heavy bruising to his face and head, was feverish and was having difficulty breathing. Like the injured men from the other glider, none of them had received any medical treatment since they had been tended by a Norwegian medic, who had got to the crash site before the Germans. The conditions in the cell were filthy.

Crow said that there was an argument between the Wehrmacht and the Gestapo about what should be done with the survivors. The Wehrmacht argued that the soldiers should be treated as prisoners of war and taken to a camp, but the Gestapo said they were saboteurs who should be executed after interrogation. Hitler, enraged by the growing success of British sabotage raids across Europe and North Africa, had passed a new order, just a few weeks prior to Operation Freshman, to the effect that all commandos were to be shot on the spot as *francs-tireurs*. The order read:

> From now on, all opponents brought to battle by German troops in so-called Commando operations in Europe or in Africa, even when it is outwardly a matter of soldiers in uniform or demolition parties with or without weapons, are to be exterminated to the last man in battle or while in flight . . . Even if these individuals, on their being discovered, make as if to surrender, all quarter is to be denied them on principle. . . . Should it prove advisable to spare one or two men in the first instance for interrogation reasons, they are to be shot immediately after their interrogation.

The British had no knowledge of the Führer's new directive and were enraged when intelligence reports confirmed it. After the conflict, the Allied War Crimes Commission invested an enormous amount of time and resources in hunting down those involved in obeying the order.

Crow, who escaped to England soon after the event, said he believed that the British soldiers were tortured after replying that they 'would not betray the honour of a soldier' to each question put to them.

Crow said the soldiers told him that their glider had been cut loose at a very great height and that they had spiralled at great speed into the rugged mountain terrain below. After tending to their wounded comrades after the crash, and sewing up those who had died in tarpaulin, the survivors had burned all their papers, but had missed a map that had marked out their route to Vemork. Not wanting to leave their wounded comrades to freeze and starve to death, and assuming they would be taken as prisoners of war, they sought out local help. Two of them set off towards Helleland and were put in touch with the local sheriff, who in turn alerted the Germans. A party from the local Norwegian Labour Service, including Lima and a nurse, reached the crash site before the Germans. Lima later compiled a report on what happened and had it passed to the British authorities. He talked to all fourteen of the survivors to ascertain whether any of them were Norwegians who could be spirited away from the crash site. The glider lay scattered in pieces and the men were lying in sleeping bags, smoking cigarettes and trying to keep warm. The injured and dead had been tended to. Lima said that after about twenty minutes a German patrol of some twelve men arrived and took all the British away, first to a farm near by and then to a camp at Slettebo near Egersund. After interrogation, all fourteen of them were taken up to woods behind the camp and shot one by one, ten hours after the crash. Each man was forced to listen to his comrades being slaughtered before it was his turn to face the firing squad.

During the night the bodies were taken by truck and dumped in a shallow sand trench. In the subsequent war crimes trial (involving General von Falkenhorst, the commander of German troops in Norway during the war), one witness testified that he was one of several men tasked with loading the bodies on to a truck. He said he was convinced that some of the British men were still warm and that he could feel their blood still flowing when they were dumped in their primitive grave. (Von Falkenhorst was found guilty on several counts, including two relating to the Freshman deaths. He was sentenced to death but this was commuted to life imprisonment – curiously, on grounds of ill health. He was released in 1953 and died in 1968.)

For the rest of the war, the Norwegians tended their graves until the soldiers were given a proper Christian burial in July 1945 at Eiganes churchyard. Union Jacks were draped over all the coffins and British soldiers formed a guard of honour before they were all buried in a single grave. School was cancelled in Stavanger and the surrounding area that day, and flags flew at half-mast.

The Halifax that had been towing the glider had crashed into a mountainside moments after the two had become separated, killing the entire six-man crew. When locals reached the crash site, they were met with the terrible sight of dismembered and charred bodies scattered among smouldering wreckage. Norwegian witnesses said the Germans later threw the remains into a bog and covered them so badly that limbs were still protruding when they left the site. After the war their bodies were also exhumed and the men were given a proper burial at Helleland after a similar ceremony.

Grouse had gone to bed on the night of the operation with a sense of disappointment, but this soon turned to despair when SOE informed them of the tragic course of events. 'It was a sad and bitter blow,' recalled Poulsson. 'Not least because the weather was splendid over the following days.'

Freshman was not just a human tragedy but a strategic disaster. Thirty-four elite troops were dead while the Germans, having discovered the purpose of the mission, set about a massive programme of refortification at Vemork. The chances of a successful operation in the future had been substantially compromised. It was also likely that the Germans would sweep the area and make mass arrests to discover whether any locals had been involved in the planning of the operation. The Grouse party were now in serious jeopardy and would have to go into hiding in the most remote regions of the Hardangervidda until the danger had passed. SOE sent an urgent communiqué to the group, telling them that it was 'vitally necessary that you should preserve your safety'. They also asked for urgent information about the strength of German reinforcements to help them put together another plan of action. 'Keep up your hearts. We will do the job yet,' the telegram ended.

The party withdrew farther into the wilderness as advised, but told HQ that two of them would continue reconnaissance operations from their new base. The arrival of winter also led them to question the advisability of mounting a similar operation, but they told London that they would be happy to carry out an attack them-selves. 'Is the operation going to be carried out by Englishmen in the same manner?' they asked. 'Skiers would be advantageous. If it would assist the operation we would gladly take active part.'

Meanwhile, the Germans launched a massive sweep of the Rjukan area to hunt down the wireless operator they were cer-tain would have been used in the Freshman operation. A report in *The Times*, from the paper's Stockholm correspondent, reported that a false air-raid alarm had been sounded in Rjukan to keep the inhabitants indoors before 200 Gestapo agents swept into the town armed with grenades and machine guns. After a series of raids lasting fifteen hours, twenty-two Norwegians were led away for interrogation, but the Germans were unable to find the man they were looking for.

Operation Freshman, the first Allied glider operation of the war, was a disaster before it even got off the ground – a plan con-ceived more in wild hope and desperation than confident expect-ation. Even if they had landed safely and carried out the operation successfully, the thirty-four soldiers plus the glider crews would have had great difficulty in evading the Germans and staying alive as they fled over 400 kilometres of frozen and hostile terrain. It was to all intents and purposes a 'suicide mis-sion' that reflected the very great sense of urgency, even panic, among the Allies about the threat of Hitler's atomic bomb pro-gramme. You are left wondering whether the planners properly understood the dangers of the Norwegian wilderness in early winter. Fully trained Norwegians could have carried the mission off, partly because they could have passed themselves off as civil-ians if they had to, but more importantly because they would have known how to survive in the climate and terrain.

Tor Nicolaysen is a mountaineer and outdoor expert who, among other ventures, takes tourists along the routes and to the huts associated with the heavy water story. His hotel, Rjukan Fjellstue, is about four kilometres from Vemork. He knows the Hardanger as well as anyone alive today, and doubts whether the Freshman party would have been able to survive. 'I am sure these men would have been able to do the job at Vemork, but I do not think they would have got away. They had no skis with them, they had had no proper training for those conditions and in November of that year the weather was very severe.'

If its members had survived the journey, carried out the attack and escaped to Sweden, Operation Freshman would undoubtedly have gone down as one of the boldest, bravest and most important coups in military history. They were hard, highly trained professionals. Tragically, they never had the chance to prove themselves.

5

Down to the Very Last Drop

The best-laid plans of the Allies to destroy the heavy water plant at Vemork were effectively shredded in the wreckage of the Freshman disaster. While the urgency of mounting an attack was now greater than ever, the likelihood of one being carried out successfully had diminished sharply. German suspicions that the British were prepared to go to extreme lengths to wreck their atomic bomb programme had been confirmed by the map, with Vemork circled, that had been found at one of the Freshman crash sites. Any element of surprise had been extinguished. The British were coming, but whether they arrived by land, air or sea, the Germans would be waiting for them in even greater numbers and behind even stronger defences.

The Germans had long thought that the heavy water cells in the basement of the plant were virtually invulnerable, protected by concentric rings of defences, both natural and of their own making. The first line of defence was the North Sea and the heavily fortified Norwegian coast. Then there were the vast expanses of forbidding terrain surrounding the approach to the Rjukan valley, with its raging winds and blood-stopping cold. The valley itself was passable only by a single road, so any raiding party mad or bold enough to approach it would now have to do so on skis and then on foot down precipitously steep slopes. If the raiders got as far as the outlying area of the plant, they would then have to find a way of reaching what amounted to an eagle's eyrie, perched on the rock face several hundred metres up a cliff. The Germans did not believe it possible for humans to scale the gorge and they based their defences around the narrow suspension bridge crossing it and the pipelines running down the cliffs behind the plant. (Today, the gorge attracts the world's leading ice-climbers, which gives you some idea of the difficulty of scaling it.)

In the unlikely event, that the British managed to infiltrate the complex, they thought, they would have to overpower the Germans inside before breaking into the basement and laying and detonating their explosive charges before German reinforcements arrived from Rjukan. As military missions went, this one seemed all but impossible. If the British thought they could carry it off, then good luck to them – this was the prevailing German attitude.

But this plan of attack, mere fancy to the Germans, was exactly what SOE decided upon in those frantic few days after the Freshman catastrophe. The only difference was that it would be carried out by Norwegians disguised as British soldiers.

SOE had been handed sole responsibility for the new operation after it was accepted that a Combined Operations attack, similar to Freshman, had become unworkable. The Norwegian section in Scotland was told to arrange for an attack party to be dropped in during the very next moon period in December. The new operation would be code-named Gunnerside. No more time could be lost, partly because it was now almost twelve months since the heavy water production at Vemork had been increased by almost thirty times its original rate, but also because they feared for their advance party camped up on the Hardangervidda.

The SOE chiefs back at headquarters in Baker Street knew that Grouse's rations would be running dangerously low, and they worried about their chances of survival during the coming winter, when all vegetation would be lost to the blizzards, ice and biting arctic winds. Herds of reindeer would soon be migrating into the southerly reaches of the Hardangervidda, but no one could predict exactly when. Meat and fat alone could not sustain the men until the spring. To survive they also needed vitamins and carbohydrates from fruit and vegetation.

Within days of the Freshman tragedy, SOE sent a message informing the party that another attack would be attempted in the week leading up to Christmas. The name of their own operation would be changed from Grouse to Swallow just in case the Germans had somehow learned of their existence during their intensive interrogations in the wake of Freshman.

They decided to abandon the Sandvatn hut and also to cease all wireless contact with England until they could be certain that the German 'razzia', the name given to the searches, was over. It was a tense situation, and Grouse knew that their best option was to go to ground until the storm blew over. Under the strict rules laid down by SOE, the Swallow party was not meant to have contact with any other agent, although both they and Skinnarland knew of the other's existence. But inevitably their paths crossed as Swallow needed assistance to carry out their duties. Skinnarland, who took away their accumulators for recharging, suggested they hide out in the Grasdal hut, which belonged to the leader of the Rjukan branch of Milorg, the Norwegian resistance. The four decided to divide up all the equipment before splitting into pairs and going their separate ways for a while.

On 23 November they arrived at the new hut with all their equipment, except the Eureka machine, which they had hidden, and then set off for their container depot at Fjarefit to collect the rest of their gear. In the dark they were unable to find the containers and were forced to burrow holes in the snow and spend the night in their sleeping bags after a blizzard had erupted across the Hardangervidda. The following day, still battling against the ferocious snowstorm, they managed to locate the containers and divide up the equipment after erecting a parachute for shelter from the driving snow.

Poulsson and Kjelstrup went to an area called Vinje, while Haugland and Helberg, loaded with as much food and gear as they could carry, headed back to the Grasdal. The former pair were literally blown apart by the power of the wind. 'We often had to crawl along on all fours,' said Poulsson. They were both forced to take refuge at nearby farms, which was something they would only do in a great emergency as they feared that rumours of their presence in the mountains could reach the Germans or the quislings in the local community. Both, though, were taken in by good Norwegians with no questions asked, and two days later they were reunited at the Grasdal hut before striking out on their own the following day.

Over the next two weeks, the four Grouse members, working in pairs or on their own, dodged the German razzia before reconvening at the Grasdal hut. It was 'remarkable', according to

Poulsson, that they had managed to escape the German sweeps. He and Kjelstrup arrived in the Rauland area the day after the Germans had been there, while Haugland had left just hours before they had arrived. Helberg had arranged to meet Torstein Skinnarland but, by the grace of God as it turned out, had been unable to make it because of the appalling weather conditions. Torstein was arrested on the day they had arranged to meet and sent to a concentration camp at Grini, near Oslo. Another of the Skinnarland siblings, Olav, was also arrested as the Germans attempted to weed out every possible pocket of resistance in the region around Vemork. Torstein's arrest was a major blow, not just for Swallow, but for Allied intelligence. Happily his brother Einar was tipped off that he too was being sought and managed to flee up to the Hardangervidda just in time. As the Germans combed the area for Einar, the Swallow party decided that it would be in everyone's interests if he lived with them until the searches were over.

Einar proved to be a superb addition to the team, and without him they may not have survived, let alone have been able to carry out their operation. He was an enormously good-humoured man and his high spirits and permanent smile helped lift the morale of the party. 'It was a pleasure to be with him,' Helberg wrote in his official notes. 'A matter of tremendous importance in circumstances so difficult as those we were in.' Skinnarland gathered information about German troop movements and the heavy water production at Vemork, brought ammunition for reindeer hunting and charged the accumulators for the wireless and the Eureka machine.

Through his brother Torstein, Einar had occasionally managed to get supplies to them. It was mainly just flour and oatmeal, but all contributions were welcome. 'Now and then he [Skinnarland] got us some extra things: dried milk, sardines, beans, oats, potatoes and other things. Such things added zest to our existence,' recalled Poulsson. But the arrest of Torstein had ended this vital supply link and the party were now forced to fend for themselves at the onset of one of the worst winters the area had experienced for years.

When he was with them at the hut, Skinnarland was a bundle of restless activity, preparing food, chopping wood and clearing up. He was also one of the best skiers in the Telemark region, an area he knew as most of us know only our back gardens. His resourcefulness and practical skills were also responsible for saving the party's contact with London. The hand-operated generator, needed to power the machines, was a troublesome piece of equipment, very heavy and with a handle so stiff to turn that it utterly exhausted anyone using it. With energy levels among the party already dangerously low, the physical burden of operating the hand generator placed an unsustainable stress on the party. On one night, the situation was desperate. The plane carrying Gunnerside was expected, but the party could not get the generator to work and thus risked losing contact with the RAF crew via the Eureka machine. Skinnarland, though, saved the day by making hasty repairs, although in the end the drop was called off.

The following day, Skinnarland built a longer handle, so that the party were able to operate the generator without exhausting themselves. His practicality had saved the day. The men were also experiencing power problems with the wireless. They could receive messages, but were unable to send any. Skinnarland, however, improvised the connection set-ups and linked the generator to the wireless. This was a turning point. Thanks to Skinnarland's initiative, Swallow were able to maintain contact with London, thus saving the operation. 'But for Einar Skinnarland's clever work, we could hardly have carried out our mission successfully,' Helberg told his British officers. 'But for him, the efficiency of our intelligence work would have been small. But for him the W/T service would very probably have broken down. But for him, we could hardly have kept going owing to a lack of food – at any rate until the reindeer hunting began. He was invaluable.' (Unfortunately the occasional loaf of bread Skinnarland had been able to procure for them caused even more problems. 'Norwegian bread always gave us diarrhoea,' recorded Poulsson.)

These were trying times for all connected with the operation. Food supplies were very low, they didn't have Eureka and they had to ascertain the strength of the guard at Vemork – a prerequisite before they could carry out any raid, but it was difficult to move around without arousing suspicions. 'We had three tasks as we waited for Gunnerside,' said Poulsson. 'The first was to stay alive, the others were to maintain radio contact with England and to establish contact with people who could give us information about what was happening at Vemork and what the Germans were up to.'

On 11 December, they made contact with England and were told to prepare for the arrival of the Gunnerside party within the week. Physically, the party were in a bad way, having eaten little and poorly over the previous weeks. When they were put on stand-by on the 16th all four had gone down with fever and severe stomach cramps. 'We all fell sick after we found some dried meat in another hut. It had been left in salt for about two months, but we made the mistake of not boiling it twice to get rid of the salt content,' Haugland recounted. 'We should have thrown out the first water. I have never been so sick, but we did not suffer for long.'

In spite of their sickness, Helberg and Kjelstrup struggled across the frozen landscape to fetch the Eureka machine from the hiding place near the Sandvatn hut. Poulsson meanwhile went out every day in search of reindeer, with his Krag rifle and some magazine cartridges that Einar Skinnarland had procured for him. The weather, though, was bad, and Poulsson could find no reindeer. To compound their misery, they had exhausted their store of dry wood. By the 19th the party was growing desperate for food, though none of them communicated their anxiety to the others.

As their powers of resistance began to fade, Kjelstrup and Helberg both developed oedema, and they swelled by about 20 pounds each. The condition, a bloating caused by an abnormal build-up of fluid in the body tissue, also meant that they had to urinate about half a dozen times per night, which only added to their fatigue. It became hard just to get out of the sleeping bags and relieve themselves. Periodically, all the party suffered dizzy spells, fevers and powerful waves of nausea.

'We soon finished all of our rations apart from a very small amount kept aside for emergencies,' recalled Helberg.

We tried to find reindeer but there were none in the area at this time because the migrating herds always head towards the wind and the wind was not blowing in the right direction. We broke into huts to take what we could find, but without much success. During peacetime people left quite a lot of basic supplies like sugar, oats or dried fish, but because of the food shortages of the war, there was very little left in the mountains.

One of the most remarkable features of Grouse's battle for survival in the most difficult conditions imaginable was the fact that they all kept their composure and sense of solidarity. No one lost his temper. Instead, they kept each other going by telling stories about their childhood, cracking jokes and looking ahead to a life free from Nazi occupation. The morale of every member of the group was essential to the success of the mission. Their mental health was almost as important as their physical health, but despite the enormous pressures they were under they managed to keep their spirits nourished. 'We were living the whole time in the mountains in primitive conditions,' recalled Poulsson. 'We never saw any new faces. The conditions were therefore present for the so-called "Polar sickness", but this was an illness unknown to us. It was just the primitive conditions we were living under that caused the battle for existence to take all our energies. We had not time to get on one another's nerves.'

The survival element and outdoorsmanship are key elements of the story about the Allied efforts to destroy Hitler's atomic bomb programme. While the area may not have the steep slopes and high peaks of the Alps or Himalayas, the gentle, rolling hills of the Hardangervidda should not deceive anyone. It is like a hugely scaled-up version of Dartmoor, relocated to the Arctic, several hundred metres higher and exposed to raging winds from the north. One of the many incredible features of the Hardangervidda is that it is less than 200 kilometres from

Oslo and the conurbations of the south coast, and nowadays no more than a two-hour flight from Britain. It lifts the heart of an outdoorsman today to know that he could take his breakfast in London or Oslo or any other European city and a few hours later could be preparing his lunch in a snowhole in the teeth of a ferocious storm in one of the last surviving wildernesses this side of Siberia and the Arctic. This is a place to test the skills of any man who enjoys the more extreme challenges that nature can offer. We should be thankful for its existence, but in that brutal winter of 1942–43 the four members of Swallow were not there for fun.

The spirit and selflessness of the Swallow men during their protracted stay on the Hardangervidda were truly remarkable. Anyone who has spent long periods of time in the wild in the close company of others will understand the practical difficulties and emotional strains that can stretch the bonds of men to snapping point.

They were never told the main purpose of their mission and they had no idea about the enormous stakes involved or the great responsibility to the Allied war effort, arguably to the very future of the free world, that rested on their shoulders. They had no idea that back in London Winston Churchill would eagerly await news of their mission, as would Roosevelt in Washington. To them this was just another task they had been asked to fulfil on the fringes of the world conflict. Despite the immense difficulties they encountered during those months, not once did they complain about their condition in their correspondence with London. Not once did they fall out among themselves, despite the desperation of their situation. It is no exaggeration to say that death, or very serious illness at the least, stared them in their gaunt faces during this period, and yet with unfailing good humour and a sense of unbreakable brotherhood they continued to push themselves to the very limit of human endurance to accomplish the mission they had been given.

'All of us could ski, all of us could read a map and use a compass and all of us could take care of ourselves in extreme weather or stay out a night in the open if we weren't able to get back to a hut,' recalled Poulsson.

There's a physical aspect but the psychological aspect is also very important because of the loneliness.

You grow to learn everything about your comrades and all their little habits, good and bad. Little things can become very big under those conditions, but I was very lucky because my men were of the highest calibre. Comradeship is very important and my men had the mentality for it. They also had great stamina. If they saw something needed doing, they just did it. They didn't wait for someone else to do it. They were all very keen and we remained very good friends throughout. If a man didn't have the right qualities, it could have made our life Hell up there.

The party moved to a hut called Svensbu (also known as Fetter) by a lake called Store Saura, and they finally managed to put something substantial in their bellies when Helberg stole some old fish, buried in the earth of a neighbouring hut. The hut turned out to be the best of all the ones they stayed in. It was hidden away and not marked on local maps, and even more crucially it was situated near a clump of birch trees which they could use for firewood. There was also a wood-burning stove that was lined with stone and allowed them to burn unseasoned wood. Here they would simply have to chop the wood and throw it in, whereas at the other huts they had to dry it out first. When possible death or serious illness due to cold and/or starvation was only a day away at times, being able to generate heat at once was an incalculable boost to their existence.

The huts were crucial to the Swallow party. In extremely cold conditions it is vital that clothes, tents and other equipment are dried out and that the body can warm up and recharge. Once a stove was lit and the floor and walls had heated up, it was relatively easy to keep them warm by placing skins over them. But to keep them warm they needed wood, and the farther they headed up from the valleys the fewer trees there were, which meant they regularly had to make back-breaking toboggan expeditions to the lower slopes. 'Wood makes you warm twice, first by collecting it and then by burning it,' they used to say, but the downside was that its collection would use up more energy, when their levels were already low due to malnutrition, the all-pervasive cold and the physical exertion from other activities such as hunting or reconnoitring. Despite the occasional difficulties of finding it and transporting it, wood provided them with hot meals and drinks and dry clothes. It was one of the few sources of physical comfort they enjoyed during that long, especially cold winter.

Food, though, or rather the lack of it, had become a major problem, nagging away at the back of their minds since they first set foot back on Norwegian territory. Half their rations from England had been consumed by the end of October, and now they were all but finished. The mainstay of their supplies was a substance called pemmican, which has its origins among the Native Americans, who were expert hunters and fishermen from the Canadian sub-arctic region. Derived from the Cree word 'pemikan', it was made up of dried meat, fat and fruit that has been shredded and pounded into a small but highly nutritious slab, perfect for soldiers' rations, and could be eaten raw or cooked in a broth. Overall, their rations were good, but the problem was the quantity of them. They had not known that they would be forced to wait that much longer before the Gunnerside party would arrive, or that there would be an exceptionally severe winter that year which would make daily life so much harder and sap them of so much energy.

With his comrades deteriorating before his eyes, and despite his own seriously failing health, Poulsson set out day after day, his Krag rifle slung over his shoulder, and skied across the great white expanse of the Hardangervidda in search of food. A man experiences a powerful sense of loneliness, insignificance and other-worldliness when he is all alone on the Hardangervidda without another human or sign of life for as far as he can see – and he can see an extremely long way on a clear day. But for Poulsson, delirious with tiredness and malnutrition, dragging himself through the snow in a desperate quest for sustenance to keep himself and his friends alive, those feelings must have been almost overwhelming.

Volcanic activity formed the bedrock of the Hardangervidda 1,000 million years ago before the Ice Age shaped it into Europe's largest high mountain plateau 9,000 years ago. Traces of civilisation there date back 8,000 years. It was Stone Age man who brought the trout to the lakes and rivers, laying the foundations for the vast stocks of fish to be found there today. Norway boasts the largest reindeer herds in all Europe, but there were none to be seen despite the dozens of miles Poulsson covered each day, weather permitting. The mountain at the heart of the plateau is like the centre of a clock around which the reindeer rotate through the passing seasons, but the time had clearly not come as Poulsson scoured the horizons.

Finally, on 23 December, Poulsson looked through his binoculars for the umpteenth time in the last few weeks and, to his heart-jumping delight, saw several dozen specks on the great white horizon. Was he seeing things in his delirium? He looked again. No, the reindeer had come at last. He did not move a muscle as he tried to work out the best way to approach these highly sensitive animals. One jerky movement or noise breaking the cold silence and the reindeer would disappear over the next horizon, not stopping until they knew they were safe from their predator. Reindeer have an extremely acute sense of smell. Poulsson was an expert hunter, and he slowly closed in on the herd without arousing suspicion, ensuring he was downwind from them so that they would not pick up his scent.

He was shaking with a mixture of anxiety and anticipation as he stole ever closer to the beasts, which had developed their white winter coats. He was excited because he could almost taste the succulent reindeer meat in his mouth, and knew that he and his comrades would survive the coming weeks if he could shoot one; frightened because if he scared them away there was no telling whether he would get a second chance, and all the men under his command were on the verge of falling gravely ill. The next hour would be one of the most critical in the lives of the four men. It was also vital to the success of the planned attack at Vemork. If the four had died or fallen so ill that they could no longer operate, SOE would have to decide whether to abort the mission, perhaps unwilling to risk six more good men without up-to-date intelligence. If they lost contact with Swallow, how would SOE know whether or not they had been captured by the Germans and talked under the Gestapo's brutal form of interrogation?

The beasts had stopped to graze at a lake at the bottom of a valley, and Poulsson found himself trapped. If he moved one way, they would see him; if he moved the other, his scent would be carried to them on the wind. He was forced to sit it out in the hope that they would work their way up the craggy hillside where he would have the natural cover to get within shooting range of them. The sun had already begun its descent and the temperature had started to fall. Unable to move without alerting the reindeer, Poulsson began to fear the onset of frostbite, and he started to pull faces in a bid to keep his circulation going. Occasionally he took his hand from his glove and pressed a point on his face which he had felt starting to stiffen. As he lay there, he also wriggled his toes and ruffled his beard to prevent it from freezing.

Two young bulls wandered away from the rest of the herd in Poulsson's direction, but they were still too far away. He had to act soon before darkness fell and before the growing cold threatened to get the better of him, despite his precautions. When the two bulls turned around and began to head back towards the others, Poulsson took a gamble and seized the moment. Leaving his skis and rucksack, he broke cover and began heading down the slope, but it was slippery and as he crashed to the ground the two bulls turned and saw him.

Immediately they threw their hind legs into the air and stamped the ground to alert the rest of the herd before they all stampeded in a flurry of snow and pounding hoofs over the hill and out of sight. 'It was enough to make a man weep,' recalled Poulsson.

He was not to be defeated, and after collecting his equipment and putting on his skis he set out on their trail once again. Reindeer do not have especially long memories, and to his great relief Poulsson soon came upon them in the next valley. This time he was in a position to get close enough to them to take a shot. He wanted to get near enough to be sure of hitting his target, but time was running out and he was starting to feel colder and more light headed as the minutes ticked by and the sun fell lower and lower behind the mountains. He hoped to shoot two of the beasts, and knew from experience that it was possible to bring the first down without alerting the others to the danger. During the winter, the Hardangervidda would often reverberate to the crack of what sounded like gunfire to the untrained ear. Poulsson had heard the noise several times over the past few hours. It was the sound of the earth cracking as it froze. The reindeer were used to this noise too, and if Poulsson could hit one with an accurate shot, there was a good chance it would fall silently to the snow, as if lying down. He would then be able to get in at least one more shot before the rest of the herd woke up to the danger and fled.

Poulsson took aim and fired. The animal didn't move an inch and his hopes were dashed at once as the flock panicked, possibly after one of them had heard the thud of the bullet in the snow. As they fled, Poulsson fired off two more shots, and within seconds the herd was gone from view and earshot. A crack marksman and experienced hunter, Poulsson could not believe he had missed with all three bullets and, close to despair, he was about to set off back to the hut when he noticed a trail of blood in the snow. Frantically he scrambled up the hill, and then just over the brow there before him he saw his prey, a young female. Dizzy with fatigue and cold, Poulsson took aim again and fired. The cow slumped to the snow. As he rummaged desperately to find the tin cup in his rucksack, he began to laugh uncontrollably, knowing that he and his comrades would feast like Norwegian kings that night and for days afterwards. They were saved. Poulsson quickly gathered the warm blood spurting from the animal's wounds and drank it voraciously before it froze. Drinking the blood is a traditional practice amongst hunters in the far north and it provided Poulsson with an instant shot of energy and warmth.

His strength partially restored, he set about skinning the animal and chopping it up. The head and tongue, Poulsson's favourite parts of the animal, were the first into his rucksack, followed by the fattiest cuts, such as the ribs, heart, liver and kidneys. To keep himself going as he finished chopping the reindeer, he chewed pieces of raw fat and drank the runny marrow from its leg bones. As the sun began to set, he covered the rest of the carcass with the reindeer's skin so he could collect it the following day. With a rucksack of prime meat and a bucket of frozen blood, he quickly set off for the hut. To carry so heavy a load in such a weak condition was an incredible feat. On his way back, Poulsson encountered another herd of reindeer, which disappeared in an instant as he struggled over the horizon, but he knew that he and his comrades would now have plenty to eat over the coming weeks. The reindeer migrated south in the winter, and the sighting of a second herd told him that they would now be on the Hardangervidda in their thousands.

Poulsson staggered back into the hut covered in frozen reindeer blood, and the other three cheered with joy. It was to be a happy festive period for the young Norwegians after all – relatively speaking, of course. 'Christmas was particularly enjoyable that year because we had such a feast,' said Helberg. 'We made ourselves a small Christmas tree, listened to music on the radio and had a fine time of it.'

Most young Norwegian boys of the time had grown up reading the books of the legendary Helge Ingstad, a pioneering trapper, polar explorer, historian and writer. Ingstad, who died in 2001 aged 101, spent long periods living among native Indians in Canada and found proof of a Viking settlement in Newfoundland. His books inspired several generations of Norwegians, and his descriptions of Indian eating habits and survival techniques were well known to Poulsson and his colleagues. It was from reading Ingstad that they knew they could eat the moss in the reindeers' stomachs and how best to cook it. 'From him I learned how to use the meat so that we could live on it exclusively without falling sick,' said Poulsson. 'We were very, very hungry and if we hadn't been able to shoot reindeer I don't think we could have accomplished what we did.'

That night, and over the next few weeks, the four of them would devour every last morsel on the carcass of the reindeer, even stewing its bones to make soup. The parts of the animal they had relished in peacetime, like the lean steaks, were no longer the prized pieces. Instead their bodies craved fat, which was essential to their beleaguered digestive systems in the absence of sugar and carbohydrate. The most favoured part of the animal became the fat behind the eyelids and the marrow in the bones above the hoofs. They would also eat the nose, lips, brains and the eyes themselves, as well as all the vital organs.

The pelts of the animals they used to cover the floorboards and the door. The bones were pulverised and boiled for forty-eight hours until they became a thick, tasty, jelly-like substance which they added to their porridge. But the part of the animal that did more than anything to keep them alive was the half-digested moss they found in the reindeers' stomachs. This was rich in vitamin C and carbohydrate, which was essential to their survival because it stopped their blood sugar levels falling to dangerously low levels. Eating fat and protein without carbohydrate is like burning a candle without a wick. The moss, which was mixed with blood and then heated up, came to be considered a 'delicacy' by the saboteurs. 'We ate everything except the balls and the hooves. The head was the best bit,' said Poulsson. 'The skins we put on the floor, ceiling and walls to make the hut warmer.'

Reindeer are the unsung heroes of this story. Without them, Swallow would have died or been forced to come down from the mountains and risk almost certain capture and arrest, which in turn would have led to interrogation and internment in a concentration camp at the very least. Torture and execution were the fate awaiting resistance fighters and British agents. The Swallow party almost certainly would have known as a matter of medical fact that their bodies needed more than meat and water to keep them going over a long period of time, and even if they didn't they would have felt their bodies crying out for carbohydrate and vitamin C like an addiction. The reindeer and its half-chewed moss saved them.

The bad news was that the party would have to wait at least another month for the arrival of Gunnerside as the weather had been so bad over the December moon period that the RAF were unable to drop the party. For the next month, the Swallow team settled into a weary routine. Their beards grew long and their skin became sallow, but thanks to the reindeer, Helge Ingstad, their own survival skills and the strength of their spirit, they were still alive.

6

Shelter from the Storm

SOE wasted no time in raising an alternative plan for an attack on Vemork following the Freshman disaster. Every day lost to the Allies was a day gained for Hitler. The heavy water stocks had been growing slowly, and at some point in the near future there would be enough of it to be shipped back to Germany and put at the disposal of the Führer's atomic scientists.

The plan was simple and decisive: an attack party of six Norwegians, drawn from the Linge Company and to be known as Gunnerside, would be dropped on to the Hardangervidda by parachute at the earliest available opportunity. After teaming up with the Swallow party, they would advance to the target, destroy it and then escape to Sweden. To some extent, SOE's decisiveness was thrust upon them by circumstance. There simply *was* no alternative. All other options had been ruled out. Bombing from the air was unacceptable to the Norwegian authorities; it was too late for a flying-boat operation, even if they decided that this was the best course of action; glider-borne troops were off the agenda after Freshman and an 'inside job' risked heavy reprisals on the local population.

The SOE chiefs knew exactly who they wanted to lead the attack party. He was a man who, physically and figuratively, stood head and shoulders above the rest, a man whose very presence inspired total respect. His name was Joachim Rønneberg, and he was just twenty-two years old. 'Rønneberg was one of the most outstanding men we had. He was well-balanced, unflappable, very, very intelligent and tremendously tough,' recalled Colonel Charles Hampton, who ran SOE's Norwegian schools in the Cairngorms.

Rønneberg, who was from Ålesund on the west coast, had recently finished his studies and was working for a firm exporting fish abroad when war broke out. 'No one had expected the invasion. It came as a complete shock,' he recalled.

> Where I came from on the west coast between Bergen and Trondheim, the Germans did not arrive in great numbers until the autumn. Then life changed completely. All the towns were blacked out and we were very restricted. The Germans were singing in our streets and after a couple of months many of us got fed up with it and decided to get out of the country and return to fight in the open rather than stay and try and be a nuisance.

> To live in an occupied country is very distressing and you have to experience it to understand. We felt that there was no sacrifice too great to get the Germans out. You have to fight for your freedom and for peace.

In March 1941 Rønneberg took the boat from Norway, squeezing into a small fishing vessel with seven other eager young volunteers. 'When I got to Britain I met Martin Linge and after talking with him for a while I abandoned any plans to join the navy and decided to join the Norwegian Army.'

Rønneberg was told that the five men he would choose to join the party would have to be expert 'ski-runners' in a state of the highest fitness. 'I was honoured to be given the job of picking my own men, but it was tough because I could have chosen twenty-five men,' he said. 'I had seen all the Norwegian chaps in training because I had been involved in much of the instruction. I wanted strong, physically fit men with a good sense of humour who would smile their way through the most demanding situations.'

Rønneberg's second-in-command would be Haukelid, who had recovered from the foot wound that had prevented him from taking part in the Grouse/Swallow operation. The other four were chosen for their intelligence and their quiet, unassuming determination, which would make them good 'team' players ideally suited for a mission that would demand stamina, bravery, discretion, technical expertise, snowcraft and survival skills in equal measure. He had got to know them well during the training programme and saw that they were the type of men who would just get on with the job without any fuss, no matter how trying the circumstances. The four he chose were Hans Storhaug, Birger Strømsheim, Fredrik Kayser and Kasper Idland.

Rønneberg knew Strømsheim from before the war when they had been members of the same ski club. Strømsheim, the oldest man in Gunnerside and Swallow at thirty-one, was a signals operator with the air force. Storhaug, an outstanding skier, was known as 'the chicken' to his colleagues after an incident with a Scottish gamekeeper during their training. He was caught plucking a pheasant he had snared, but escaped before the gamekeeper could apprehend him. The gamekeeper went to SOE to complain about the poacher and when asked whether he could identify him replied: 'Of course I can, he had a great big beak and looked just like a bloody chicken!'

The SOE chiefs summoned the six volunteers to underline the great risks involved in the operation and stressed that they were likely to be killed if they were captured following Hitler's new directive about the treatment of British commandos. 'We went down to the Norwegian section of SOE in London where Professor Tronstad told us about the Freshman operation and all the terrible details of the disaster,' Rønneberg recalled.

> They told us everything – that those who had survived the crash were shot, or 'experimented' on, and that some were thrown into the North Sea. They told us that we would be given poison capsules so that we would not have to suffer the same ordeal.
>
> He never mentioned what heavy water was for and no one ever mentioned nuclear weapons. I certainly hadn't the faintest idea that Churchill was taking an interest in the raid. But you understood it had to be very important because it was impressed upon us that the raid had to be carried out as soon as possible before the Germans could build up their defences. There was no time to lose, he told me.

After months and months of training, all six men were already in peak physical condition when Rønneberg singled them out to join Gunnerside, but their ski training, so vital for building up the right muscles, had been limited as the Scottish winter was only just beginning. 'Fortunately I had had quite a lot of experience of the outdoor life, climbing and skiing and living in the wild, but some of the Norwegians weren't outdoorsmen who knew the mountain life,' said Rønneberg.

Some were fishermen, others were from the towns. For them the training was a great help, learning to map read and survive in the open and so on. To start with it was probably a bit too demanding for some of the chaps but after three weeks most people had adapted. The collective spirit of the recruits was a major element. We picked each other up and you realised very quickly the importance of working as a team. During the training very strong friendships were formed which last to this day.

The most pressing priorities were to acquaint the party with the layout of the Vemork plant and the heavy water apparatus they would find in the basement there and to show them how best to blow it up. The six men were transferred to STS 17 at Hatfield in Hertfordshire, which had been evacuated of all other 'students' in order to maintain the utmost secrecy. Here, under the supervision of Tronstad and Brun, an exact up-to-date replica of the Vemork heavy water room had been built, and the sabotage party practised laying explosives on the cylinders, often in the dark. All six were made to carry out the exercise over and over again until they could do it at great speed and without even having to think about it. 'Jomar Brun had arrived in Britain bringing with him very detailed drawings of the plant and as a result of it I can confidently say that no sabotage operation launched from Britain into occupied Europe at this time enjoyed better information than ours,' said Rønneberg. 'I was even told where to find the key for the lavatory to lock up the Norwegian guard. None of us had been to the plant in our lives but by the time we left Britain we knew the layout of it as well as anyone.'

During the week the group were also given intense physical

training as well as shooting practice with Colt. 32s. (One evening during their training the six men were handed new firearms as they wound down at the end of another day. Five minutes later the sound of gunfire could be heard coming from the room and the instructor rushed in and saw a hole in the wall. 'What the hell is going on?' he snapped. To which Rønneberg replied calmly: 'We are just testing our new weapons and mine appears to work.')

Owing to the haste with which the Gunnerside operation was put together, their parachute training at Ringway near Manchester was pitifully brief. 'We had three jumps, that was all,' said Rønneberg. 'One individual jump, one group jump and one night jump.'

Rønneberg was meticulous in his planning, and he realised that success or failure, even life or death, could hinge on the smallest details. 'We were made to do much of the planning of equipment for the operation ourselves, which was good because it kept us busy and focused and stopped our thoughts wandering about what might happen and so on,' he said. 'We were a little astonished when we were told that we would be wearing British battle dress and not our Norwegian uniforms during the operation and withdrawal, but they explained that we would probably receive better treatment if we were caught.'

The British uniform was of excellent quality and would serve them well, but finding other equipment suitable for operations in a Norwegian winter was more difficult, given the shortages of supplies during the war. The operation planners at SOE understood that the Norwegians themselves would have the best idea of what they would need for the mission and so they gave them the money to buy much of their own personal equipment.

Sleeping bags would be essential, as the group would almost certainly have to spend several nights outdoors in temperatures of minus 30 degrees Celsius during the withdrawal to Sweden. On 10 December, Rønneberg took his men to a bedding manufacturers called Hamptons Ltd in London's Knightsbridge area. 'From there we were sent by taxi to their factory down in the docks, where we explained as vaguely as possible that we were Norwegian soldiers training in the Cairngorms and needed a very special kind of bag,' said Rønneberg.

> I remember he was a very helpful man and said that even though he had never made a sleeping bag in his life he was willing to try if we gave him some details. So we scribbled some diagrams and tried to explain what we were after. We were surprised when we came back the very next day and the man rolled out a sleeping bag which he invited us to try out there and then.
>
> It was almost exactly what we wanted and it needed only a few minor alterations – they needed to be a bit bigger because we would be wearing full uniform with our boots and hats on. There also needed to be a small slit in the hood of the bag through which we could breathe. The man also finished it off with some waterproof material, which was vital.

Weighing only five pounds and taking up little space when rolled up, the bags were perfect for a Norwegian winter and would provide good warmth in a snow hole provided they prepared their beds properly with branches and heather underneath their groundsheet.

Realising that footwear was going to be essential when they

began their long, arduous trek to the Swedish frontier during the coldest months of the year, Rønneberg ordered some specially made boots from a firm called R. Lawrie & Co., based in Newark, East Midlands. The pair they were initially issued with were found to be hard wearing but not watertight, while the standard British pair afforded good protection against water penetration but were not so durable. 'I managed to get some good boots for the party after a chance encounter trekking up in the Cairngorms,' recalled Rønneberg.

> I bumped into two students and couldn't help but notice the quality of their boots. They gave me the name of the manufacturers. It was a great stroke of luck, because on a hard march you needed the best footwear.
>
> Our skis came from the Norwegian stores depot at Dumfries. Most of them were Norwegian but there were also some Canadian ones too. Snow goggles were also vital. You can't go out in the mountains without snow goggles because you get badly sunburnt and it feels like you have a kilo of sand in your eyes.
>
> We also knew from our training that we would need the most powerful weapons possible because we imagined we would have to fight our way into the plant and out again. So we chose the Colt revolvers and tommy guns partly because they used the same ammunition but also because they were really good 'stopping' weapons.

At the end of Gunnerside's training Major Rheam at SOE wrote in his report: 'This was an excellent party in every way, and each member has a thorough knowledge of the target, and the methods of dealing with the different sections. Their demolition work was exceedingly good and thorough and their weapon training out-standing. If the conditions are at all possible, they have every chance of carrying out the operation successfully.'

Like Swallow, Gunnerside were never told about heavy water. Their precise orders read as follows:

i) The enemy is utilising the power available at Vemork for large scale experiments of a highly secret nature which it is judged essential to bring to a standstill. This entails the destruction of the finishing stages of production.

ii) Gunnerside will attack the storage and producing plant at Vemork with high explosive, so that present stocks and fluid in the course of production are destroyed.

iii) The leader will bear in mind that the stocks of fluid in the basement are the main target, and these must be destroyed regardless of the remaining target.

The party would be met by Swallow at the landing place, but if that was not possible then they would meet at the Svensbu hut at the earliest opportunity that the weather or security precautions allowed. Together they would make dumps for their equipment which they would collect before setting off on their withdrawal. The two parties were to advance to a forward base close to the target before a final reconnaissance trip was made. If, on the basis of that recce, Rønneberg considered that the raid would have no chance of succeeding, then the party were to withdraw and await further orders. Any Norwegian guards encountered at the plant were to be gagged and bound. German guards would be 'put out of action as circumstances demand'. While Gunnerside withdrew to the Swedish border after the raid, the Swallow party would melt away into the Hardangervidda according to Poulsson's orders. No contact was to be made with Norwegian civilians unless absolutely necessary. Quislings were to be executed and the saboteurs were to make clear to any others they encountered the 'grave consequences' of exposing them (i.e. they would be killed by the resistance). Special care was to be taken to avoid farms where children could be seen or where there was a telephone. The use of public transport was strictly forbidden.

The party was scheduled to be dropped in the moon period beginning on 17 December with a view to carrying out the attack on the night of 24/25 December, when festive celebrations made it likely that the Germans would have dropped their guard. Before heading back to Scotland, the Gunnerside group were sent to STS 61, a large country house near Cambridge where they were lavishly entertained by FANYs. A common practice of the War Office was to give 'special forces' soldiers an all-expenses-paid night out before their operation. The FANYs were first-class hostesses and were fondly remembered by all the members of Grouse/Swallow and Gunnerside. They were also highly professional operatives and would be watching for any signs of indiscretion or weakness in the young soldiers they took out on the town. They also ensured that they did not talk to strangers after a few drinks.

Before they left, Professor Tronstad gave the Gunnerside men a moving pep talk in which he evoked the memory of those who had died in the Freshman operation: 'You must know that the Germans will not take you as prisoners. For the sake of those who have gone before you and are now dead I urge you to make this operation a success. You have no idea how important this mission is, but what you are doing will live in Norway's history for hundreds of years to come.'

The following day the six men were taken to an airfield, ready to be flown out, but like Swallow before them they were to be frustrated by dreadful weather conditions over the coming days, and the mission was postponed for another month. The sense of anti-climax they experienced presented a 'severe trial of nerves', according to Haukelid. They had completed their training, received their brief, packed their equipment, focused their minds and steeled themselves for the challenges ahead only to spend long, anxious days sitting in a safe house waiting for the weather over the North Sea to clear. The Norwegians came to refer to Britain, especially Scotland, as 'home' throughout the war, but during these waiting periods there was little comfort their adoptive country could offer them.

After the December drop was aborted, Gunnerside were taken back to one of SOE's stately homes in England, but Rønneberg soon demanded that they return to hard physical training in Scotland. The Gunnerside leader wrote to Tronstad to complain that the training they were doing on the lower ground in England was unsuitable for their mission. 'The muscles used when running on roads and fields are not the same as used when marching in broken and hilly country ... Perhaps it would be possible to send us up to one of the schools in the Arisaig area.' The Norwegians loved the training they received in Scotland, where the conditions were as close to those they would find on the Hardangervidda as anything Britain could offer. Although it was nowhere near as cold as Norway, the cold in Britain is challenging, being 'wet' because the temperature rarely falls below minus five and there is still moisture in the air. Norwegians, and others from more northerly climates, are always surprised by how cold they feel in Britain, even though the temperature is markedly higher than in the drier conditions they are used to.

Despite the setback and their poor physical condition, the Swallow party, back on the Hardangervidda, immediately set about making preparations for the arrival of the six members of the Gunnerside party during the January moon period. Einar Skinnarland was detailed to get the accumulators recharged and gather the latest information about German troop strengths at Vemork. Poulsson and Kjelstrup were to team up with Haugland after he had dropped the accumulators, and together they would go on to fetch the remaining containers. Helberg was to collect the equipment he had left at earlier hideouts, then shoot reindeer and lie low.

By the time Poulsson and Haugland had returned to Svensbu, having found the containers, the temperature had plunged. 'The weather was splendid,' recalled Poulsson. 'But it was awfully cold.' On the inside walls and ceiling of the hut, the hoar frost lay deep. They did not know it at the time, but the Telemark region was experiencing one of the most severe winters on record, and the temperature rarely rose above minus 30 degrees Celsius that January and February. Only around the stove was there any degree of warmth. Swallow were meant to make contact with England on 9 January, but Poulsson had been unable to fetch the accumulators until the 13th. Unfortunately, they had not been properly charged and lacked sufficient acid. With the wireless reception growing weaker, Skinnarland, the only one allowed to leave the hut during the stand-by period, was dispatched to fetch the hand generator. The toing and froing between various huts and hiding places for equipment was a logistical nightmare, but an imperative one as they could not risk having all their equipment in one place. Moreover, it simply wasn't physically possible for the party to carry all the equipment with them at once.

Like Gunnerside back in Britain, the four men of the advance party were as bored as they were frustrated by the long waiting period between the full moons. Helberg occupied himself by making a number of reconnaissance trips into the Rjukan area. On each occasion he had to resist the temptation to pay a visit to his family and friends or to try to acquire vital food supplies to supplement their reindeer diet. 'Once I skied past two friends of mine, but they were good Norwegians and they said nothing. They didn't even tell my father,' Helberg recorded. He would often make his excursions under cover of darkness, and used to sleep in a small hut right next to his family home. But not once did he walk the few dozen yards to their front door and make contact. Throughout the entire war, the Helberg family thought their son was in Britain.

On 23 January Swallow finally received the crackle on their wireless set they had been waiting for – the signal 211. Gunnerside were on their way at last. Like their comrades in the advance party two months earlier, Rønneberg's men set off in the bright moonlight towards their homeland, and as they flew over the coast they were soon able to look down and see their compatriots outside their houses and driving along roads. The weather was perfect, but they circled over the Hardangervidda for over an hour looking for the lights laid out by Swallow. As the navigator tried to pinpoint the exact dropping zone, the six Norwegians, their stomachs taut with nerves, sat ready to jump through the uncovered hole of the Halifax.

Swallow turned on Eureka, but almost immediately it began to run out of power. They were just about to give up hope when Skinnarland arrived with the hand generator and the homing device was quickly restored to full power. Around midnight they heard the drone of an aircraft and quickly put on all the lights, but the aircraft disappeared in a westerly direction and there was not a crackle or squeak from Eureka. At three in the morning, exhausted and disconsolate, the team resigned themselves to the painful fact that yet another attempted drop had been aborted.

The RAF pilot's report on the flight stated that they were unable to find the exact pinpoint at the first attempt, and then returned to the area only to overshoot it. They saw what they thought was Lake Møsvatn but could not be sure because the ice on it appeared to have altered its shape. At no point did they see the reception lights that Swallow were meant to have laid and there was no contact via the Rebecca/Eureka system. 'Passengers [i.e. Gunnerside] were asked whether they could recognise the ground near pinpoint but were unable to do so. ... Passengers were satisfied that there was no reception,' the pilot noted.

When the fuel situation became urgent, the pilot turned round and returned to Kinloss. Deflated and irritated, the Gunnerside, laden with their heavy packs, felt the wheels of the aircraft bounce on to the runway. Another month of waiting lay ahead of them.

There was a general reluctance to criticise the RAF, which lost men in their thousands conducting sorties behind enemy lines, but according to the minutes of the meeting held to discuss the aborted mission, the plane's navigator was given a dressing-down for not being able to pinpoint the exact dropping zone during that period. SOE also argued that the men should have been dropped at another suitable location because they were roughly in the right area. Whoever was to blame for the latest failure, it was another crushing blow to the party to have flown over the area on a perfect cloudless night only to have to head back to Britain for another whole month before the next moon period. Time was running out. In a few months' time, the long nights would start to become long days and there would be no chance of flying at all. Tensions were building within SOE and within the Gunnerside group itself.

It was now over three months since the Swallow party had leapt from the aircraft and readied themselves for the arrival of the raiding party. Were their comrades ever going to come? And if so, how much longer could they hold out against the weather, malnutrition and the enveloping net of the Germans trying to track the moles in their midst? To make matters worse, over the days that followed the aborted mission Haugland fell very sick and Poulsson developed a painful inflammation on his left foot. Snow bound and bedridden, the advance party for one of the most important sabotage operations in military history had ground to a frozen, painful standstill.

SOE feared that the latest failure could have a devastating effect on the morale of the four men, and they sent a message trying to lift their spirits: 'Deeply regret weather conditions have made it impossible to land party. Do hope you can manage to keep going until next stand by period February eleventh to twenty fifth 2200 to 0200 GMT. We all send you our thanks and admiration.'

Poulsson, too, was full of admiration for the men under his

command. These were severely testing times and, as his log notes make clear, he was deeply impressed by their fortitude and professionalism. Of Helberg he recorded: 'A worker, as hard as nails. A man who never spared himself. On account of the circumstances, the heaviest jobs fell to his lot. Always in good humour, always willing.'

Of Kjelstrup, the Swallow leader said: 'Clever and careful, never attracted attention to himself in spite of the fact he had chronic stomach trouble.' Of Haugland he wrote: 'Excellent W/T operator. Knew his job thoroughly and able to work under most trying conditions.'

On 1 February Gunnerside returned from England to Scotland and stayed at a house belonging to Major McKenzie of SOE in Kilfinan, Argyllshire, on the shores of Loch Fyne. Here they continued their heavy physical training in the surrounding mountains with full packs ('Excellent country', according to Rønneberg). When the February full moon period began, the six-man party was once again put on stand-by for another attempted drop. It was a measure of the urgency of the situation and the frustration of the Gunnerside party that at the next attempt they would be dropped without trying to make contact with Swallow on the ground, and whether or not the RAF crew were able to pinpoint the designated dropping zone. 'We told them not to bother about the reception committee at all and that once we were on the ground we would find our own way,' said Rønneberg.

Once again, the Norwegians packed up their equipment and checked it over and over again to make sure nothing had been overlooked.

Each man had been issued with the following:

Equipment worn for parachute jump:
String vest
rabbit-skin jockstrap
woollen vest, pants, stockings and socks
British Army uniforms including a khaki shirt, scarf, battledress
    'blouse' and trousers
wrist-warmers
snow gaiters
ski boots
woollen mitts with trigger finger
wind-proof gloves
balaclava
khaki ski cap with peak
handkerchief
braces
boots with big socks

To be carried in pockets at jump:
Swedish-model compass
map of south Norway (scale 1:100,000)
Norwegian kroner
notebook and pencil
lighter
matchbox
snow goggles
wristwatch
48 hours' worth of rations
pistol holster and Colt .45

2 reserve magazines
large knife
suicide tablet

Additional clothing in rucksack:
Thick Islander pullover
khaki finger gloves
gloves with trigger finger
spare socks and bootlaces
handkerchief
camouflage suit
down sleeping bag
groundsheet
enamel cup, spoon
2 Tommy cookers

General equipment for whole party:
2 Primus stoves
2 cooking pans
2 paraffin tins
10 packs Meta fuel
5 first-aid packs
toilet equipment including razors, shaving brush and soap,
  soap, toothpaste, toilet paper (one packet), towel, toothbrush,
  comb
3 sets field glasses
2 map holders
2 complete sets of maps
snow goggles
3 torches + 12 sets of batteries

Orilux torch
candle lights
dubbin
petrol lighters
matches
waxed thread (for shoe repairs)

Skiing equipment:
1 pair Canadian skis per man
Norwegian bindings
Norwegian sticks
ski skins
30 tins ski wax
2 spare ski tips
2 toboggans
2 repair kits

Rations:
150 'man day' rations
600 ascorbic tablets
10 poison capsules

Weapons:
5 Thompson (tommy) machine guns + 20 magazines with 1,000
    rounds
.303 sniper's rifle with 50 rounds of ammunition
10 Colt .45 pistols with 500 rounds of ammunition
10 hand grenades
12 chloroform pads

Booby-trap equipment:
10 primers
4 pull switches
4 rolls tape
4 rolls wire
2 boxes detonators

Explosives equipment:
4 sets of 9¼ lb charges
6 Bickford initiators
2 jemmies
12 coils of tape
6 pairs rubber gloves
12 30-second fuses
4 fireman's axes
2 pencil time-fuse tins
3 detonator magazines
12 striker boards
12 primers
6 torches
10 special charges
2 Cordex (explosives)
6 boxes of fuses
6 wire-cutters
1 pair double-mouthed cutters

The rations consisted of 250 pemmican biscuits, 20 kilograms of sugar, eight of oats, eight of chocolate, eight of butter, seven of dried fruit, two of tea, two of cocoa, 10 pounds of cheese, ten tins of dried milk, 7 pounds of flour, 20 tins of corned beef and an unspecified amount of tobacco and cigarettes.

Today we have equipment that is much more lightweight than that of the Gunnerside party, but otherwise what they took would be broadly similar to what a good outdoorsman would take now (minus the weapons and explosives). The same principles still apply: natural fibres like wool are different to synthetics. Wool is particularly effective in an environment like the Hardangervidda because it keeps you warm as it dries and you can live in it for weeks without it becoming rank and unhygienic in the way that synthetics do. The clothing the Gunnerside party took was ideal, as good as or even better than anything you could find today.

The volume and weight of their kit, however, were a problem. If you have 30 kilos of equipment on your back and you are dragging a heavily laden toboggan weighing at least twice that across broken terrain in freezing conditions, the strain on the human body is immense. A good outdoorsman knows that it is very important to travel as light as possible, for the obvious reason that it allows you to conserve energy, but this was not an option open to Swallow and the Gunnerside parties, who had weapons, explosives, weeks of rations, cooking equipment, tents, extremely bulky and cumbersome wireless machines and generators, as well as piles of other equipment vital for their survival and mission. To transport that amount of equipment in any conditions would be extremely hard going, but to do so under extreme weather conditions and in a debilitated state is a feat of the greatest physical endurance and mental toughness.

Once the two convalescents, Haugland and Poulsson, had recovered some of their strength, the party once again went about the business of preparing for a freshly attempted drop. Such was the success of Skinnarland's improvised hand generator that they decided to do away with the bothersome 12-volt accumulator which had proved so unreliable, as well as a risky nuisance to get recharged through contacts in the Rjukan valley. Skinnarland was due to return with the other accumulator, but had collapsed on his way back and lay helpless and feverish in a hut called Grunnos.

The only good news for the party during these long, frozen, dark days was that for much of the time there was little they could do but go to bed. Often they would sleep up to fifteen hours at a time, and in that way they were able to preserve what strength they had. 'During the long wait for Gunnerside we would often go to bed at six o'clock to save the fuel for the light and because there wasn't much else to do once it got dark,' recalled Helberg. 'We just lay in our sleeping bags and each of us would give talks on different subjects. I would talk about the mountains and how some of the peaks had come to get their names. We would talk about anything to pass the time. Arne Kjelstrup, who was a plumber, used to tell us all about plumbing!'

But the long winters nights took a heavy toll on Haugland, whose scheduled transmission and reception times meant he had to haul himself out of his sleeping bag in the middle of every night. 'At one-fifteen in the morning I had to get up and call the station while my three friends lay in bed snoring,' he recalled.

It was fortunate that on the last occasion I had been in Stockholm I had bought myself a small alarm clock. Sometimes there would be two or three separate messages and I would spend an hour or two in the cold and dark trying to decode them in case they were of vital importance.

I worked by a single candle light and the following morning I would always have a terrible headache because the light was so bad on my eyes. It was often very, very cold at night but I could not transmit with my gloves on because the different style of my transmission made them suspicious back in London and they feared that my station had been taken over by the Germans. I also had to make contact at nine o'clock in the morning, so the nights could be very tough going.

Mistakes were common among W/T operators working under extreme pressure behind enemy lines, but only once during his entire stint on the Hardangervidda did Haugland appear to err. He was strongly rebuked for using an erroneous coding system while sending an urgent message in haste when his fingers were numb from the cold. The operators back in England grew familiar with the idiosyncratic styles of their operators in the field, and there was something suspicious about this message. Some operator's dashes and dots were shorter or longer than others and each one's 'fingerprints' were recorded and filed at HQ, so that they had a chance of telling whether the sender was really their man in the field or whether the message was being sent by the Gestapo, which had captured him.

SOE had suffered a disaster in the Netherlands when their agents had been captured and for over a year they were sent false information by the Germans. Fearful of another disaster they sent Haugland a pre-arranged security message: 'What did you see walking down the Strand in the early hours of January 1, 1941.' Haugland replied: 'Three pink elephants.' There was palpable relief back at HQ, but Haugland was not amused by the suggestion that he had made a mistake.

Utterly confident about the quality of his transmissions, he sent back a stinging reply which read, 'Astonished about your telegram – are only following best W/T rules for English wireless communications – our telegram about landing place is quite clear – ending is correct as in the other telegrams.'

On the very day they were put back on stand-by, 11 February, a ferocious storm descended on the Hardangervidda and it was impossible to move even a few metres outside the door of the hut without getting blown over by the biting wind. They had spent many a winter's day up here as schoolchildren and young men, but none of them could recall one as severe and relentless as this. The storm brought with it the risk that once again the arrival of Gunnerside would have to be postponed, leaving just one more window of opportunity for a drop in March before the nights would become too short for the RAF to operate.

As they boarded up the hut and tried to keep as warm and active as possible, their only consolation was that as the storm raged there was no chance of the Germans venturing out to find them. They were protected by the best defence known to man – Nature herself. The Swallow party had come to regard the Hardangervidda as their own back yard, a small corner of an occupied land that would be forever Norway. The Germans could stay for a thousand years but they would never take the Hardangervidda. Swallow did not fear the Hardangervidda; they showed it respect and bowed to its natural authority. If the wind howled, they stayed in their hut or buried themselves in a snowhole until it had abated. They did not try to tame the Hardangervidda because there was no point. There would only ever be one winner.

They used the Hardangervidda to their advantage against the Germans. First and foremost, it was, so long as they were careful, an impregnable hideaway. There was always the danger of being spotted by a plane or a patrol during one of the occasional sweeps of the area, but even then they had a good chance of slipping farther into the wilderness, where the Germans would dare not venture. Second, it served as their pantry or local store, providing them with reindeer (food and pelts), firewood, bedding (branches and heather) and water.

On 16 February, 1943 the weather cleared and Gunnerside were airborne again, leaving the airbase at Scotland at around 2000 hours. It was fine and clear as they approached the Hardanger, and at two minutes past midnight Rønneberg was given the green light to plunge through the dispatching hole and into the frozen night. He jumped from just 700 feet, and the other five men and their eleven equipment containers followed in rapid succession, forming a spectacular sight as their chutes opened and they floated down towards the immense white expanse below.

The dispatcher's report read: 'Exit according to plan and in perfect order. Highly successful with men in good spirits.' The rear gunner counted all seventeen chutes opening and the pilot, Squadron Leader Gibson, confirmed that contact with Swallow's Eureka machine had been made (Swallow, curiously, claimed there had been no contact).

Three months after being told they had been chosen for the mission, the six young Norwegians finally felt their homeland beneath their feet and rolling bodies. At last, almost three years since the night their country was invaded, they were in a position to strike back at the enemy and play a part in the struggle for its liberation. But as they thumped, one by one, into the snow and ice of the Hardangervidda hillside, there was no time to reflect and enjoy the long-awaited moment of their return. The containers were littered all around and they needed to gather them up quickly and set out in search of their comrades in the advance party, of whom there was no sign as they floated to earth.

They could only watch as one of their containers, holding three of their rucksacks, was dragged two kilometres by its parachute. It finally got wedged in an ice crack and the party were able to rescue it. 'We were lucky because if we had lost the rucksacks, half the party would have had no equipment and the operation would have had to have been postponed. We were tremendously lucky,' Rønneberg later said. One sleeping bag and two of the rucksacks were damaged but the rest of their equipment appeared to have landed safely. The party unpacked their kit and buried under the snow everything that they didn't need for their advance or for the attack itself. They placed stakes in the snow and took orientation bearings so that the gear could be recovered at a later date.

By four o'clock they had finished sorting out the equipment and were ready to move on. Rønneberg asked Haukelid where he thought they were. 'We could be in China for all I know,' came the reply as they stared out at the frozen, moon-like expanse around them. This was an entirely different planet to the one they had been living on for the last twelve months or so. Throughout that time, in spite of the hard training, they had lived in the cushioning knowledge that a vast support network, in the form of the British Army and the Scottish people, had fed them, housed them, clothed them and entertained them. It wasn't luxury, just basic human comfort, but now, twelve hours on, they were standing in the middle of one of the most desolate environments on earth with nothing but their own wits, stamina and some basic rations to sustain them.

Moreover, they were now deep in enemy territory, three or four hundred kilometres from their only feasible means of escape, the Swedish frontier. It was strange and galling for them to reflect that they were now strangers in their own country, prey for a ruthless predator. There were around 300,000 German troops occupying their homeland – there would be 400,000 before the war was over – but the Norwegians at least had the comfort of knowing that even a million of them would struggle to ensnare them up here in the Hardangervidda. For Gunnerside, as it had been for Swallow, the Hardangervidda was now their first line of defence, a natural comrade, albeit a demanding and occasionally bad-tempered one. 'We learned that one cannot defy nature, but must adapt and accommodate oneself to her,' Haukelid said. 'Nature will not change; it is man who must change, if he is to live in conditions where nature is dominant.'

While the others raced to collect their equipment, Storhaug, the best skier in the party, had set out to try to find some shelter for the night, but returned without having found a hut. By then the weather was starting to deteriorate sharply and a violent snowstorm swept across the plateau, quickly reducing visibility to just a few yards and making it impossible for them to march any significant distance against the driving wind and snow. Although it brought the benefit of covering their tracks, this was just what they didn't need so soon after their arrival. They didn't know exactly where they were yet, and the advance party was not there to guide them to shelter.

After two kilometres of a desperate battle against the elements, with the conditions worsening by the minute, they enjoyed an enormous stroke of luck when they quite literally stumbled into a hut called Jansbu. 'We didn't even see the hut. We just walked into it – again, we were very, very, lucky,' said Rønneberg. They quickly broke the lock with a jemmy and hurried out of the biting wind. Inside there was bedding and plenty of dry firewood and the party were able to dry out and warm up as the storm battered the little wooden house.

Each man took it in turns to do sentry duty in shifts of one and a half hours, although there was little hope of their being discovered, for the storm grew in intensity as the morning wore on. 'You felt as if the whole cabin was going to be lifted off the ground,' recalled Rønneberg. The winds were still raging when they rose from their beds and looked outside to discover that two feet of snow had fallen while they were asleep and that the drifts around the hut were as high as five feet. Their training in Scotland had been of the highest order, but nothing in their experience there could have prepared them for the most extreme conditions of their homeland.

The party did not know exactly where they were, but they figured that they had landed by a lake called Bjornesfjorden. At 1700 hours they decided to set out for the Svensbu hut, but the powerful westerly wind and driving snow made the going very difficult and they could not be entirely sure that they were heading in the right direction. Moreover, they were carrying rucksacks weighing 30 kilograms and dragging two toboggans with over 50 kilograms of gear on each. An hour into their advance, the drift snow was becoming so deep that Rønneberg ordered the party to return to Jansbu.

'The order for return most probably saved the whole party

from disaster,' he noted. As it turned out, the storm continued to rage for a further six days, and the party would almost certainly have perished had Rønneberg not given the order to pull back. While taking refuge in the hut, Rønneberg worked out that they were not by Bjornesfjorden after all, but by Skrykken, some 30 kilometres north-east of the intended drop zone. It was a small, greasy thumbprint over one point on a map they found in the hut which had aroused Rønneborg's suspicions. After turning the hut upside down they found a 'Fishing Log-book for Skrykkenvann' confirming his hunch. The Gunnerside had no W/T equipment and so it was impossible for them to make contact with SOE back in England or with Swallow.

Although it was no longer snowing and the skies were clear, over the coming days the raging wind continued to drive the snow across the plateau with such a ferocity that they were unable even to venture outdoors, let alone consider resuming their march. Also the sudden and dramatic change in climate conditions led to two of the party falling victim to heavy colds, making them feverish and swelling their glands. Swallow, who had been informed by London that Gunnerside had landed, were now beginning to fear the worst for their compatriots. They knew better than anyone that unless they had brought a tent with them they would be in serious difficulties. 'This storm was much worse than any we had experienced so far. It just went on and on for about a week and we became very anxious for Gunnerside because we didn't know if they had found a hut or were managing for food,' recalled Helberg.

There was disagreement about what the Swallow party should do. It was suggested that an expedition party should be sent out to Bjornesfjorden as soon as the storm abated, but Poulsson was resolutely opposed to this. His reasoning was that if the pilot had been unable to find the intended drop zone, which was well marked, he could have dropped them anywhere.

On the fourth day Gunnerside attempted to return to the depot where they had buried the rest of their equipment in order to fetch more rations, but they were driven back by the storm. 'While waiting for the storm to pass we used all the rations we had taken in our rucksacks and we then had great difficulty in finding the store depot we had made because the snow had completely altered the landscape,' said Rønneberg. That night, the wind reached such force that it blew the chimney pot off the hut. 'I twice tried to climb on to the hut to fix it but on both occasions I was lifted up by the force of the wind and thrown into a snowdrift on the other side of the hut.'

The following day they tried again, but the drift snow was so deep that the stakes they had driven into the snow had been completely covered and the visibility was so bad that they could not even read their compasses to get their bearings. After three hours, they once again abandoned any hope of finding their cache and, exhausted and ravaged by hunger, they returned to the Jansbu hut.

On 21 February, Rønneberg recorded in his notes: 'The snow storm raged with renewed power. Visibility was zero. The general lassitude of all members of the party was still very much in evidence, and two men were seriously ill from colds.' To make matters worse, they discovered that some of their ration containers had after all been damaged in the drop. Packets of salt had broken and spread amongst everything else, making it taste disgusting. The rucksacks with the food had been poorly packed for them back in Scotland and two of them were a mess of different foodstuffs with broken biscuit, margarine, sugar and raisins all mixed up among socks and gloves.

In his notes, Rønneberg registered his anger about what he saw as the haphazard packing of the various containers. But his complaints were later dismissed by Colonel Wilson, the head of SOE's Norwegian section, who pointed out that each container was clearly labelled to explain what it included – one for explosives, one for spare clothing, etc. What had happened was that the packers, with the best of intentions, had tried to do the party a favour by squeezing in as much extra food as possible anywhere they could. The row may sound like a petty squabble now, but it was a matter of the greatest significance to the men of Gunnerside, who needed every last morsel of their rations to keep up their strength and energy.

On 22 February, the storm finally blew itself out and the exhausted, battered Gunnerside party awoke to clear skies and fine weather. All was now peaceful on the Hardangervidda, which had become a giant expanse of brilliant white stretching as far as the eye could see. Every rock, peak or shrub had been blasted with snow, which gave the landscape an eerie, otherworldly atmosphere.

The march to Kallungsjå on the way to the Svensbu hut was going to be steep and hard going, and with his men in such poor condition Rønneberg decided that their loads should be reduced to a minimum. Taking British uniforms for the Swallow party as well as equipment and five days' worth of food and the explosive equipment, they set out at 1300 hours, each carrying rucksacks weighing 25 kilograms and pulling two toboggans of 30 to 40 kilograms.

Just as they were about to set out, to their alarm the party spotted a figure making his way towards the hut. It was unlikely to be a lone German out on patrol, but it might well be a quisling informer. The man was seized and taken into the hut for interrogation. Like Swallow, the party were under strict orders to kill anyone with whom they came into contact who might compromise the successful execution of the operation. Or as Rønneberg put it: 'If necessary we could liquidate him in the mountains.' This was a wholly unwelcome development for the party. Did they compromise the operation by letting this man go or did they kill him, even though he might be a true Norwegian? 'It was a very difficult decision, whether or not to shoot a man whose only fault was to be in the wrong place at the wrong time,' noted Rønneberg.

The man was Kristian Kristiansen, a 43-year-old reindeer hunter, and he was in possession of a rifle, which had been banned by the German authorities. He was also carrying a large quantity of cash and a list of customers in Oslo. The man was a profiteer – and these soldiers and patriots did not like that. During the interrogation, a complicated game of bluff and double bluff developed as neither the hunter nor the Gunnerside party wanted to blow their cover and reveal the wrong hand. The hunter thought that the party were members of the Hird and so tentatively suggested that he was a supporter of the NS (Quisling's Nazi party), although not a member. Rønneberg decided to make use of the man and made him guide them to Kallungsjå while pulling one of the toboggans. During the march, Rønneberg began to feel that the hunter could probably be trusted and may not have to be killed, but he still wasn't sure. His head said kill him, his heart said let him go. Whatever else he may have been, Kristiansen turned out to be a guide and skier of the very highest order, working every lie of the undulating land to their advantage.

At four in the morning, after four hours' march, they reached a lake called Hettefjorden, where they rested until sunrise. On reaching Kallungsjå, shattered by their arduous trek, they caught sight of two men, both with beards, skiing hard across the near horizon. Haukelid was ordered to swap his camouflage snow suit for civilian overclothes and to make contact with them, telling them if necessary that he was a reindeer hunter. The rest of the party took cover behind boulders or lay flat in the snow, clutching their tommy guns and pistols. It was another anxious moment for Gunnerside as they watched Haukelid and the two men tentatively approach each other. To Haukelid, the two men looked like tramps. Their clothes were filthy with reindeer blood, their beards long and scraggy and their faces emaciated, yellow and sickly. But then, as Rønneberg recalled, 'A wild yell from the three told us that we were in touch with Swallow!' It was Helberg and Kjelstrup, who had been sent out by Poulsson to search for the raiding party the moment the weather had cleared. Poulsson's deduction that the new arrivals would take the route via Kallungsjå had been proved right. 'It was a great moment but I was struck by how thin they were and how long their beards had grown.'

There was much back-slapping among the eight men. 'We greeted each other with as much emotion as Norwegian men can,' said Helberg. But there was still the question of what to do with the reindeer hunter. In the end, it was decided to release him, but only after taking precautions against him blowing their cover. As security, they made Kristiansen sign a declaration that he owned the rifle and they told him it would be handed over to the German authorities if he failed to hold his tongue. (The Germans threatened the death sentence for anyone found carrying a rifle to shoot reindeer. In a further bid to prevent resistance cells forming in the mountains they also banned all forms of outdoor equipment such as tents and sleeping bags.)

As an added measure, they gave him rations for five days, hoping that the supplies would persuade him to stay in the mountains long enough for the operation to have been completed before he returned to civilisation. Thoughtlessly they also gave him some English chocolate. An agent's cover could easily be blown by the smallest detail of their clothes and belongings. A pair of pants with a British label or design, British tobacco scraps in a pocket, a pencil – all of them could lead to the execution of an agent in the field. So scrupulous care was taken to ensure that every last item of their equipment could be explained away if necessary. To this end, various factories, laboratories and workshops were set up by SOE and the other secret services to produce goods and materials suitable for each occupied country. The chocolate they gave to Kristiansen was a grave oversight.

At around four o'clock in the afternoon Poulsson looked anxiously out of the Svensbu hut and saw Helberg approaching dragging a toboggan – and he realised instantly, to his joy, that the two parties had found each other. Before greeting Gunnerside and following SOE's strict procedures about avoiding contact with fellow operatives, Skinnarland was immediately sent away before they reached the hut. Exhausted and half starving, Gunnerside had covered 45 kilometres in sixteen hours, and it was with unbridled relief that they collapsed among the company of their compatriots.

That night the ten men enjoyed a rare feast. They were all in poor condition after their different ordeals, although Poulsson, curiously, recorded in his official log that he and his men were in excellent condition. Gunnerside, he said, were 'not acclimatised and pretty done up'. If that were so, and Swallow having been described as 'emaciated and sickly' by the new arrivals, it gives us an idea of the parlous state Gunnerside were in after their eight-day ordeal on the Hardangervidda.

Reindeer, of course, formed the centrepiece of their banquet in the wilderness, but Gunnerside were also able to produce chocolate and dried fruits. After indulging their appetites, the men sat around the wood stove, smoking cigarettes (Poulsson puffed on his pipe) and chatting about their various experiences over the previous months. For the Swallow party it felt as if they had been shipwrecked on a desert island over the previous four months, but now they were able to catch up with news from the outside world, the state of the war and the fate of mutual friends. The following day, they knew they would return to the more serious business of planning one of the most audacious sabotage raids in military history, but chocolate, tobacco and storytelling were the order of that night.

In the morning, Haugland sent the following gleeful message to London: 'The party arrived yesterday evening. Everything in order. The spirits are excellent. On the air again after the operation. Heartiest greetings from all.' The Gunnerside party rested that day, trying to recover their strength ahead of the raid. Helberg, meanwhile, was dispatched to Rjukan, where he was to meet a contact to get the latest information on German troop activity and defences at the plant. Haugland dismantled his wireless and set off for the depot at Skrykken, collecting Skinnarland along the way. The two would now lie low and wait for their colleagues to deposit a message at a pre-arranged rendezvous giving them details of the attack to transmit back to England. For the other nine, there was just forty-eight hours to go before they launched one of the most daring coups of the Second World War.

7

The Raid

The members of Swallow had had plenty of time over the long winter months to consider the best possible route for the parties to take to launch their attack on the plant. They decided it would be impossible to go straight down the near-vertical mountainside on the other side of the narrow valley to the plant, and it was absolutely out of the question to try to return by that route. They pinpointed the Fjosbudalen hut as the best starting point for the attack as it was close to the plant and yet seldom visited by people. Also the descent to the Vestfjorddalen below was an easy one, compared to the other options. Rønneberg, who automatically took command of the operation from the moment the two parties met, bowed to Poulsson's knowledge of the area and that part of the plan, the descent to the valley, was agreed.

Operation Freshman had alerted the Germans to the threat of a possible attack at Vemork and a number of measures were taken to beef up security. In December the Austrian soldiers based at the plant, many of them second rate and some recovering after being injured on the Russian front, were replaced by a German detachment. The garrison at the nearby Møsvatn dam was increased from ten to forty while four anti-aircraft guns and a network of searchlights were installed. Two D/F signals tracking stations were set up, suggesting the Germans knew that a secret transmitter was in operation somewhere in the vicinity, but they neglected to make a proper search of the surrounding mountains. This was probably, in part, due to the ferocity of the 1942–43 winter, but also because they lacked men with the experience to move into the mountains. By January all the local garrisons had been increased with 200 troops now based in Rjukan and thirty at the Vemork plant, plus about two dozen near the Møsvatn dam.

On the 25th, the two parties set off for the hut at Langsjå. Despite extremely poor visibility and driving snow, Poulsson guided them expertly to the hut, owned by a Rjukan storekeeper. Metal shutters and thick locks barred their entry when they arrived at about six o'clock in the evening, but using the shears Rønneberg had bought from a Cambridge ironmonger's they forced their way in to discover a hut so well stocked with food and paraffin that they did not have to use up any of their own supplies. There was even a bottle of malt whisky.

The following day the raiding party moved up to the hut at Fjosbudalen. They were now just five kilometres or so from Rjukan, a town with a population of 5,500, which was spread over about three kilometres up the narrow, winding valley along the banks of the River Maana. Now that they were out of the barren wilderness of the Hardanger, the chances of coming into contact with other people were that much greater. But nobody, as far as they knew, had spotted them during their march. They blacked out the windows and covered every crack to avoid being detected. The hut, in a remote valley not far from the Møsvatn road, was about 800 metres up on the edge of an extremely steep slope from where they could see the long, winding town of

Rjukan, but not the Vemork plant itself, which was hidden from view by a turn in the valley.

Shortly after their arrival they spotted a man skiing towards the hut next door. He was immediately brought in and interrogated. After all they had been through, the last thing they needed was to be exposed on the eve of the attack, but fortunately, according to Rønneberg, the skier was 'recognised by one of the men as an old schoolmate and it was maintained that he was perfectly dependable. He was given the strictest orders to keep his mouth shut and, of course, never to mention his meeting with his schoolmate.'

The final details of the attack had yet to be decided. From their intelligence-gathering they knew that there would be fifteen German soldiers in the hut barracks next to the plant, plus another dozen or so billeted near by. Two guards patrolled the suspension bridge across the gorge leading from the only road through the valley. These guards would be changed at exactly midnight. In the event of the alarm being raised, three patrols would comb the factory area while floodlights would light up the vicinity around the plant and the road. Occasionally, two more Norwegian guards operated inside the factory area itself.

Crucial decisions needed to be made.

The only access to the plant from their side of the valley was by the suspension bridge straddling the gorge. If they fought their way across, then they would also have to fight the soldiers billeted in the barracks next to the plant. Once any shooting began, the Germans would immediately call up the troops based at Rjukan and Møsvatn just a few kilometres away. But even if they managed to lay their explosives while the covering party kept the Germans pinned down, their chances of escaping afterwards would be slim and they would be summarily shot by their captors – no doubt after some traditional hospitality in the Gestapo interrogation rooms.

The only other alternative was to try to climb the gorge a few hundred metres down from the plant and break their way in without disturbing the guards. They would then either return the same way or fight their way across the bridge and disappear back into the wooded slopes whence they had come. But where would they be able to cross the rapidly thawing Måna river that swept through the floor of the dark, narrow valley? And, if they managed to get across the river, how would they reach the plant, perched amid the rock and ice halfway up the other near-vertical slope of the valley? As far as anyone knew – and the Germans were convinced of this – it was not possible to scale the gorge without the use of specialist mountain equipment. But the beauty of this plan, if it worked, was that they could leave most of the equipment at the hut and travel light so they could escape more quickly. More importantly, the chance of a gun battle in which casualties would be highly likely was greatly reduced. It was also to their advantage that, as the Germans considered it impossible to enter the plant compound by any route other than the suspension bridge, the guards would not be looking out for anyone coming directly up the cliff face.

Either way, assuming they managed to break into the basement and overwhelm any guards they encountered, they would need time to strap the explosives to each of the eighteen canisters of heavy water. This would take anything up to thirty minutes depending on events, and they would then have two minutes to flee after the fuses were lit. They could assume that the subsequent explosion would immediately wake the whole garrison and the saboteurs would then have to fight their way to the safety of the mountains, where they would be the subject of a major hunt for days and weeks to come. This was the most likely course of events.

For all nine men to escape would be a major achievement. With giant searchlights sweeping across the narrow, steep valley and troops fanned out around the plant, it is difficult to see how the saboteurs thought they would have any realistic chance of getting away. They would not be able to escape behind the Vemork plant because the slope was too sheer, so they would have to fight their way across the bridge or climb back down the gorge, cross the river, climb the other, less steep side of the gorge, cross the main road and then set out on a back-breaking near-sheer ascent of the other side of the valley whence they came.

It would take them about three hours to return to the hut and all the time the Germans would be scouring the side of the slopes knowing that the attackers would be unable to take the road, the only other way out of the valley. But if – and it was a big 'if' – they managed to get out of the valley, their chances of escaping would increase dramatically. They would be back on the Hardangervidda.

It wasn't quite a suicide mission, but it wasn't far off. Whatever the chosen plan of attack, the men were going to need all their natural stealth, composure and physical strength, as well as the skills they had learned from SOE. But they would need more than that. They needed the gods on their side. One mistake and they were as good as dead. 'Our chances of being trapped in the valley were very great indeed and so we had a long discussion about the best plan for our retreat,' recalled Rønneberg. 'We knew that this was going to be serious and that we might not come through it.'

Also preying on their minds was the discomfiting knowledge that if they were caught and their Norwegian identities revealed, then the Germans would be sure to exact severe reprisals on their compatriots in the neighbourhood. For Helberg and Poulsson, whose friends and family were living just a few kilometres down the road, this was an especially heavy mental load to carry.

At 0900 hours on the day of the scheduled attack, Helberg was dispatched on a final reconnaissance trip to see whether it was possible to climb the gorge. Using his knowledge of the valley, as well as aerial photographs supplied by the RAF, it was his responsibility to mark out the saboteurs' route. He returned five hours later, reporting that the ice on the river was breaking up but there was one point where it might still be possible to cross. He insisted that they could climb the gorge despite its sheerness and even though the party would be weighed down with rucksacks full of explosives, ammunition and other equipment. He had noticed that a few hundred metres along from the river crossing point there was a stretch of small trees and shrubs working its way up the cliff. If trees could climb the gorge, so could men, Helberg reasoned. He climbed it himself to prove he was right, but he was not carrying a heavy machine gun or a heavy rucksack full of explosives, so there was still room for argument.

'I wasn't expecting Helberg to succeed in climbing the gorge but he had a big smile on his face when he came back,' Rønneberg said. 'This was great news because we now knew we could get in without alerting the Germans.'

In the official reports of the raid, and in various accounts given later, there are a number of contradictions about who was in favour of fighting their way out and escaping quickly and who wanted to retreat by the gorge without a firefight but with the risk of becoming trapped. As events would bear out, this was a crucial moment in the operation. In his official notes in the SOE files, Rønneberg says that he and the Swallow leader, Poulsson, the two most senior men in the group, wanted to fight their way out across the bridge because it offered the quickest form of escape. He wrote: 'In my opinion, and it was shared by Jens Poulsson, Alternative 1 was better in spite of the danger of loss at the bridge, taking into account we had two sick men and our loss of form.' The others were not so convinced and, although the two party leaders had the power to overrule them, they decided to put the two plans to the vote. Only Rønneberg and Poulsson voted for the bridge option; five voted for the gorge plan and two said they were indifferent. And thus, according to the highest principles of democracy, the route was agreed.

For the next few hours, the party silently went about their final preparations for the attack, cleaning their equipment, going over their instructions, checking their equipment, reviewing their proposed escape. The passwords they would use were:

First man: 'Piccadilly?'

Second man: 'Leicester Square.'

The use of torches or lights was strictly forbidden for the advance and the withdrawal. Guns were to be carried for use but not loaded until necessary to avoid the risk of accidental fire.

The group were split into two: a covering party led by Haukelid and consisting of the Swallow members Helberg, Kjelstrup and Poulsson, and the demolition party led by Rønneberg and including Strømsheim, Kayser, Idland and

Storhaug. Their operational orders covered every possible even-
tuality. 'If fighting starts before the High Concentration [heavy
water] plant is reached the covering men shall, if necessary, take
over the placing of the explosives. If anything should happen to
the leader, or anything to upset the plans, all are to act on their
own initiative in order to carry out the operation. If any man is
about to be taken prisoner, he undertakes to end his own life.' If
they failed in their mission, they would almost certainly be dead
within a few hours, either in action or by execution. Moreover,
their failure would leave the Allies with just one realistic option:
a massive bombing raid, which would almost certainly leave
dozens of their compatriots dead.

Then Rønneberg ordered them to rest for two hours, to preserve as much strength as possible for what was the greatest challenge of each of their lives. The nine Norwegians were about to
take part in one of the most important sabotage acts in the
history of warfare. They were unaware that back in London
Winston Churchill and senior figures in the government and the
military were anxiously awaiting news of the raid.

The weather was overcast, mild and very windy when the nine
saboteurs, all wearing British Army uniforms and carrying
British papers, left the Fjosbudalen hut at 2000 hours to start
their descent to the bottom of the valley. Between them they were
armed with five tommy guns with ten magazines, three Colt .32
pistols with six magazines, seven Colt .45s with fourteen magazines and ten hand grenades, two separate sets of explosive
charges and fuses and a small amount of food.

What they didn't want was a still night with a bright moon
overhead, as it would be far easier for the enemy to see or hear

them. But the wet snow, as deep as three feet in some places, made it hard going, and they were forced to put their skis over their shoulders and descend on foot, often sinking up to their waists in the deep drifts. As they approached the Våer bridge on the main road they were forced to dive for cover when two buses carrying the night-shift workers up to the plant suddenly appeared from around a bend. When the party reached the power line, they hid their skis and rucksacks before crossing the road and continuing their descent to the river at the bottom of the valley.

It was only a hundred metre drop but the heavy thaw made the surface very slippery and the ice was fast disappearing from the river. As Helberg had reported, there was just one place where they could cross, and even that had three inches of water on its rapidly thawing surface. The ice creaked and cracked as they stole their way across to the safety of the shadows at the foot of the cliff on the other side. The ascent was easier than they had expected, but with their hearts pumping with fear and excite-ment and their equipment weighing heavy on their backs and shoulders, the raiders were dripping with sweat as they hauled themselves up, clutching branches and icy ledges of rock. One slip and they would be dead. Below them lay only sharp rocks and solid ice. Never look down, they were told during their SOE training in the Cairngorms. By the time they crept on to the flat railway line that had been dug out of the rock face to serve the plant they were soaked and panting like retrievers. As they scrambled across the rails to seek cover, they noticed several sets of footprints in the snow, telling them that German soldiers had been there not long before them.

There, just a few hundred metres ahead of them, perched on

a rock shelf halfway up the side of the dark valley, sat the giant forbidding monolith of the Vemork plant, two vast stone constructions dwarfing a scattering of outhouses, including the German barracks and guards' huts. The silence of the valley was broken by the deep humming and rumbling of the giant machinery being carried along the valley by a vigorous wind from the west. For Helberg and Poulsson, it was a particularly moving sight. As children they had observed the construction of the giant complex that was to bring employment and relative prosperity to the remote community. How could they ever have imagined that a few years later they would be back here dressed as British commandos, laden with guns and explosives, poised to blow it up? A couple of miles down the road, their families lay asleep, blissfully unaware that their sons and brothers were about to risk certain death for the wider cause of Norwegian freedom and the triumph of good over evil.

Below and in front of them they could see the guards pacing up and down the suspension bridge at the foot of the winding road leading up to the plant. In the barracks next to the plant, more German soldiers were sleeping or playing cards. It was a quarter to midnight.

On the stroke of twelve the guards were relieved, just as their intelligence reports had said they would be, but they waited another thirty minutes crouched in the darkness before making their next move, working on the assumption that the alertness of the new sentries would slowly diminish. The party ate the small amount of food they had taken with them while Rønneberg went to every man individually to check they knew their instructions to the last detail. Planning was everything. A single moment of absent-mindedness could mean disaster. 'When we were sitting there just waiting it was curious because it felt more or less like we were on a short rest during a training exercise in Scotland,' recalled Rønneberg. 'Occasionally somebody told a story or made a joke, and if we wanted we could have laughed or shouted at the top of our voices because the wind was so strong that no one would have heard us. Everybody seemed incredibly calm and it was during these moments that I felt a great confidence that we could carry this out successfully.'

At exactly 0030 hours, they advanced towards their objective.

All nine crept silently to a store shed about a hundred metres from the giant wire-mesh gates. The covering party took up their positions clutching their tommy guns, while one man ran forward and snapped the thick chain lock using Rønneberg's wire-cutting shears. It took just one cut and a few seconds to break into one of the most strategically important institutions in the entire theatre of the Second World War. As the chain slackened the covering party poured forward, rushing inside the compound and taking up fresh positions. They were all carrying chloroform in their pockets to overwhelm any guards they found on patrol. The demolition party, meanwhile, forced open a second gate, ten metres below on the level leading to the basement, where the high-concentration heavy water cells were positioned.

The factory rumbled but otherwise all remained quiet. The only cause for concern was the bright moon, which had broken out from behind the clouds, and the lights from inside the factory, which had been poorly blacked out. The darkness they cherished had deserted them. The covering party took up their allotted positions close to the hut housing the German guards. Leaving one man on guard, the remaining four members of the demolition party split into pairs, as planned, with each carrying complete sets of explosives lest one team should fail to reach the heavy water. They headed straight to the cellar door, but finding it locked they tried a second entrance on the floor above; that too was secured. (The cellar door was meant to have been left unlocked by one of Skinnarland's contacts at the plant, but he had fallen ill and was unable to come to work that day.) There was no sign of Germans inside the factory.

There was only one option left if they were to avoid a firefight and that was through a narrow cable shaft Professor Tronstad had told them to use as a last resort. Thank heavens for the meticulousness of the professor! Sure enough, it was open just as Tronstad had said it would be. When Rønneberg looked round only Fredrik Kayser was at his shoulder, the other pair (Idland and Strømsheim) having got separated from them during the search. Conscious that every minute was now crucial, Rønneberg and Kayser climbed a short ladder and crawled as silently as possible down the shaft on their hands and knees over a mass of wires and pipes, pushing their sacks of explosives ahead of them as they went. Through an opening in the ceiling they could see the target beneath them. At the end of the tunnel the pair quickly slid down into an outer room before rushing the nightwatchman inside the high-concentration area.

They immediately locked the doors and Kayser held his gun to the nightwatchman, who was quivering uncontrollably. He had probably never seen a British Army uniform and he certainly would not have expected to see one here. Rønneberg tore open his rucksack and began placing the sausage-shaped explosive charges on each of the cylinders, which, down to the very last detail, were exactly the same as the models they had used in the reconstruction back in Britain. Rønneberg had laid about half of the eighteen charges when he heard a shattering of glass, and he spun round to see Sergeant Birger Strømsheim climbing in through a window from the back of the plant. Kayser also swung round and prepared to load his gun before he realised they were in good company. It was an alarming moment, and only height-ened the mounting tension they all felt as they rushed to com-plete their task. Strømsheim and Idland had been unable to find the cable duct and, unaware that Rønneberg and Kayser were already inside, had decided to take the only route left to them. It was a brave but risky move. The noise of the shattering glass might well have alerted the Germans to the raid. Rønneberg cut his hand as he rushed to remove the rest of the jagged glass so that Strømsheim could get in.

Outside the broken window Idland kept watch as Strømsheim helped Rønneberg secure the final charges and then checked them over twice while his leader laid the fuses. Originally, they planned to set two-minute fuses, but fearing that someone inside the plant might undo their work, they laid two extra thirty-second Bickford fuses as a precaution. This was a brave move because it meant that the alarm would be raised before they were out of the plant complex. Rønneberg's appetite for a fight with the Germans was remarkable, his com-mitment total: first he wanted to fight his way across the bridge, now he took another option for the good of the operation, which he had every reason to believe would lead to a blazing gunfight.

Just before they lit the fuses, the guard said, 'Please, I need my glasses. They are impossible to get in Norway these days.' It was a surreal moment and the request stopped the three raiders in their tracks, bewildered by this change to the script, this brief snapshot of civilian anxiety at the critical point of a crucial military operation. There followed a few curious moments as the saboteurs politely rummaged around his desk for his glasses. '*Takk*,' thank you, said the smiling guard as he put the spectacles on his nose. As he spoke, the four of them heard the sound of footsteps approaching. They loaded and cocked their guns and waited. Was this one of the German guards making his rounds? To their relief, a Norwegian civilian night foreman walked into the room and almost fell backwards as he saw what appeared to be three British commandos and his colleague with his hands above his head.

Outside, the covering party were growing twitchy. Twenty-five minutes had passed since the demolition party had disappeared into the shadows of the great building.

As Rønneberg lit the fuses, Kayser counted to ten before ordering the two civilians to run upstairs as fast as they could. The raiders then rushed out of the steel cellar door into the night. When they were no more than about twenty metres away they heard the dull thud of the explosion. The sound was muffled by the noise of the power station and the thick concrete walls, and the covering party wondered whether the demolition party had laid the charges properly. But Rønneberg knew from the sound that the cylinders had been destroyed and that about four or five months' production of heavy water would be awash on the basement floor, flowing towards the drains.

Unknown to the saboteurs, the sound of a dull thud in the plant was not uncommon to those who worked or lived at the Vemork installation. Small, harmless explosions in the combustion machinery could occasionally be heard, while cracking ice or a heavy collapse of thawing snow somewhere along the steep slopes could also generate a similar noise. 'The explosion itself was not very loud,' recalled Poulsson. 'It sounded like two or three cars crashing in Piccadilly Circus.'

The demolition party immediately took cover, waiting for a reaction from the German barracks hut. They lay or stood stock still as the door of the hut swung open and a soldier appeared, only half dressed, flashing a torch around the factory yard. He walked slowly in the direction of Haukelid, who was hiding behind some empty drum casks.

When he was five metres away he stopped and swept the beam of the torch no more than a few inches above the Norwegian's head. Had it been a windless night, he might have been able to hear his heavy breathing, if not the rapid hammering of his heart. At that exact moment, a range of weaponry was pointing straight at the back of the unsuspecting German. A couple of inches lower with his torch and he would have been riddled with several dozen bursts of Allied firepower. But he turned on his heel and walked slowly back to the hut, and as the door shut the order for withdrawal was given.

The restraint shown by the party underlined their great composure and utter professionalism. In one of the post-operation reports circulated between various military and political departments, the following tribute was paid to Haukelid's sangfroid: 'The exemplary fire control exercised by the leader of the covering party when the German came out within a few feet of him to see what was going on and returned to his hut, was a noteworthy feature of the attack.'

The plan was going better than the party could possibly have hoped. Only three of them had been seen – by the guards in the basement, who had no reason to suspect that they were anything other than British commandos who could speak Norwegian. Rønneberg and Kayser had made a point of showing their stripes, and they also left English tools and papers as further evidence of their 'nationality'. To avoid reprisals, it was highly important that the Germans be convinced that the sabotage had been carried out by British troops, not a local resistance cell.

The party had accomplished their mission, now they had to escape – and fast. The problem was that there was no possibility of a rapid exit from the steep Rjukan valley. It was vital that they got as far away from the plant as possible before the alarm was raised. The nine men scrambled back down the gorge and crossed over the river, which was now much higher and flowing much faster than it had been two hours earlier. Several more inches of water were now flowing above the ice, and in another hour or so, possibly just minutes, their crossing place would have been swept away altogether, leaving them stranded with no hope of being able to reach the other side. The rise in temperature and the thawing of the snow were known to the locals as a '*føhn*' and could cause havoc for the party as they tried to escape. Deep wet snow was the last thing they needed as they tried to make a quick getaway, but they could feel it squelching under their boots, as well as a warmer wind against their faces.

As they crossed the river, the whole party jolted as the apocalyptic sound of the sirens wailed out of the loudspeakers around the plant. They quickly scrambled up the bank on the other side of the river. 'The first car heading up from Rjukan came very slowly up the winding hill road, in first gear the whole way because the road was so slippery. As it passed we hid behind the snow wall created by the plough to clear the road,' recalled Rønneberg. After it had passed they ran across the main road through the valley (the only road) and recovered the skis and equipment they had hidden there earlier. As they looked back towards the plant they saw lights moving along the railway track from where they had broken in. Over the next few minutes there followed a stream of lorries and cars, all driving as fast as the conditions would allow before turning left and crossing the suspension bridge on their way up to Vemork. The race was on.

For the next three hours they struggled up the zigzagging path alongside the route of the cable car, which had been constructed so that during the dark days of winter the locals could escape the gloom of the valley floor and enjoy some sunshine on the mountain top. It was a hard climb – especially so for those in the party who were still suffering from heavy colds – because patches of bare rock made it impossible for them to use their skis. Throughout this back-breaking endeavour, the saboteurs could hear the rush of traffic in the ordinarily quiet mountain pass. They also thought they heard the crack of a rifle close to where they had crossed the main road. Curiously, the valley remained steeped in darkness. Where were the dreaded searchlights which, they were told, would sweep the surrounding area from the roof of the plant? The Germans, meanwhile, were convinced the attackers were still somewhere in the plant. They knew they hadn't crossed the suspension bridge and would have been unable – and not mad enough – to try to climb the cliff behind the plant or descend it into the gorge. They must still be inside the compound, they reasoned.

Most of the route up the steep slope, known as Ryes Road, was covered by a fairly thick covering of pine trees, but each bend in the winding path jutted out into the open near the mountain railway's cables. Thus every few minutes during their three-hour slog, the fleeing party put themselves in full view of anyone who might be looking for them there. To the saboteurs, this was the most obvious way out of the valley, but in the panic and confusion after the alarm was raised the Germans neglected to consider how the raiders might have planned their escape. The Norwegians' worst fear was that the Germans would have the wherewithal to light up the cable car and send a search party up to the top. It would have taken just minutes to rouse the cable car operator from his house close by and send dozens of troops to the top. That scenario would have spelt the certain end of their escape, because even if they emerged triumphant from the ensuing gun battle, their location would have been exposed and it would only be a matter of time before planes would have been scrambled and reinforcements from the local garrisons would have been summoned to close the net around them.

But this never happened, and at 0500 hours, exhausted but relieved, they staggered to the top. As they scrambled on to the plateau they encountered the full blast of a westerly wind blowing across the Hardangervidda, the force of which almost sent them tumbling back over the edge. They stared back at the valley below them while the Germans continued their frantic searches. As they stopped to rest and take some refreshment, they were all aware that by getting out of the valley undetected their chances of escape had just increased dramatically.

'It was a wonderful feeling because we had been concentrating on this job for many months,' recalled Rønneberg.

It was a beautiful morning as we watched the sun rise. The sky was lit up in a lovely red colour and we sat there in silence eating chocolate and raisins and looking across the valley at the Gausta mountain peak. A bird was singing in a tree telling us that spring was on its way. We were all very, very happy. Although we said nothing as we sat there I think we all felt great pride. But we also spared a thought for our British friends who died in the gliders disaster. They were unlucky, but someone was definitely protecting us that night.

The Germans were down in the valley below, but we were not that worried about them now. From now on our struggle was with Norwegian nature. But we didn't fear the struggle because we had already learnt from experience that sometimes you just have to give in and accept that nature is our master. If we paid it our respect we knew we would be all right.

They could not rest for long, though, as they needed to put as much distance between themselves and their pursuers as possible. The wind was blowing hard as they set out for the hut at Langsjå, and as dawn broke their new fear was that they would be spotted by German aircraft combing the area. The planes would either strafe them with machine-gun fire or report their position for ground troops to surround them. They reached the hut at 1100 hours, not having heard the drone of a single aircraft. They had not slept for over thirty-six hours and they had been moving as fast as their weary legs would carry them. Adrenalin had been coursing through their bodies from the moment they had set out on the raid at eight o'clock the night before. These were fit, tough men, but there is only so much punishment the body can take. They were all completely worn out, and it was with immeasurable relief that they collapsed inside the hut and tucked into more rations.

The operation to date had been a hundred per cent success, better than they could possibly have imagined during the planning of it. They had broken into the plant unnoticed, blown up all the heavy water cylinders, escaped without a shot being fired, let alone a man being lost or injured, and they had got well clear of the plant before the alarm had been raised. Furthermore, they had accomplished their mission without damaging any other part of the plant, thus safeguarding it as a vital economic interest.

The German garrison was certainly guilty of great blunders and oversights during the critical few hours directly after the raid. The saboteurs had been as lucky as the Germans had been incompetent.

The feeling that the gods were on their side that night was compounded as they lay in the hut, replenishing themselves and resting their aching limbs and muscles. For over the next hour, the wind began to blow harder and harder, and an almighty blizzard surged across the Hardangervidda. There was no chance of them leaving the hut. Just to breathe they had to put their hands over their mouths. The snowstorm would, however, cover any tracks the attackers had left in their retreat. This was a crucial development, because now the Germans would not have the faintest clue how they escaped. Had they found the Norwegians' footprints heading up the mountainside or spotted their ski trails from the air, then there would have been a very real chance of capture. Now there was simply no trace of them. They had as good as vanished into the frozen air. The Germans would now have to spread their resources over an extremely large area – over western Europe's largest and most desolate landscape.

Still, a successful escape was by no means guaranteed. Anything might happen. They might have a chance encounter with a German patrol or a Norwegian quisling, or they could be spotted from the air. But at least they would now be taking on the pursuers in their own back yard and on their own terms. This was Norwegian territory, and the Norwegians knew how to use it to their advantage.

The storm had also given the party the chance of a long rest. The only downside was that the lull gave the Germans time to call up massive reinforcements from neighbouring garrisons in the full knowledge that the raiders too would have been paralysed by the storm and would still be within a few kilometres of Vemork. They were out there somewhere.

The following morning, 1 March, the party set out for Svensbu, but the ferocity of the storm forced them to return. By the afternoon the wind had eased a little and they set out again at 1700 hours, reaching the relative safety of the hut at 2130 hours after battling through driving snow and a wind that had returned to its earlier intensity.

Back at the plant, Alf Larsen, the chief engineer at Vemork (and one of Swallow's main contacts inside the plant), was among the first at the scene of the sabotage. 'When I got through the door I could see that all the high-concentration cells had been blown up and the bottom had been knocked out of each individual cell. The whole room was full of spray, which was obviously caused by shrapnel from the explosions having penetrated the water tubes to the plant. It was like standing in a shower. This was a perfect sabotage act.'

General Wilhelm Rediess, the head of the Gestapo in Norway, arrived at the plant to inspect the damage and discover how the 'impregnable' plant had been breached, by whom and to where they may have fled. He was not in the best of moods that Sunday morning. Rediess wanted answers and he threatened reprisals. He accepted that the raid had probably been carried out by three British commandos. A tommy gun had been found along with other British Army effects, and the two guards who had been surprised inside the plant backed up the conclusion (though it is not clear whether they knew that the raiders were actually Norwegians but didn't let on for fear of reprisals). The broken padlock, open gate and trail of footprints (and blood from Rønneberg's dripping hand) revealed their approach and escape route, but they remained baffled as to how the saboteurs managed to negotiate the gorge. Rediess was convinced that the raid could not have taken place without inside information, and although he suspected that the former manager, Brun, had supplied it, he immediately ordered the arrest and interrogation of engineers and laboratory assistants, threatening to have them shot unless the mole was revealed.

It was only the arrival of the Wehrmacht general von Falkenhorst which prevented Rediess from having his way. Von Falkenhorst was one of the few high-ranking Germans to emerge with any credit and humanity from the Vemork story (though he would later be convicted of war crimes related to other incidents, including the Freshman operation). He declared the sabotage act to be 'the most splendid coup I have seen in this war'.

According to a telegram sent by Haugland, Skinnarland's contacts at the plant had told him that von Falkenhorst had even smiled when he first laid eyes on the damage and saw the quality of the saboteurs' work. 'British gangsters,' he muttered. Intercepted messages between the Germans and Norwegian intelligence showed that the enemy believed the three Norwegian-speaking men had come by train to Rjukan dressed as civilians, but must have had local knowledge. Curiously, the fact that they knew the raiders spoke 'perfect Norwegian' did not arouse suspicions. But once von Falkenhorst had declared that the attack had been a military action not involving locals, the Germans released the detainees and a massive man hunt for the *Britischers* was launched. Locals would later express their appreciation of von Falkenhorst standing up to the Gestapo's insistence that reprisals should be meted out to the local population.

While he was trying to establish how the raiders had managed to escape, von Falkenhorst ordered the German guards to switch the floodlights on, but to their embarrassment, and his anger, they were unable to do so because they couldn't even find the switch.

There were now eight men in the withdrawal party, Helberg having left them to return to the hut at Fjosbudalen, where he had left his civilian clothes and the faked Norwegian identity cards for his reconnaissance trips. It was important that these were not discovered by the Germans, as reprisals on the local population would certainly follow. Before he set out on his own he arranged to meet them again at Svensbu as soon as the weather – and the Germans – made it practicable.

On 2 March, the main party left Svensbu and set out for Skrykken, where Gunnerside had landed, but once again they were forced to beat a retreat in the face of a severe storm, this time two hours into their trek. The following day they had more success. En route they diverted as planned to Slettedal, where they hid a message for Haugland and Skinnarland, the W/T operators, who would pass the details back to HQ in England. It read as follows: 'Landed Skrykkenvann. Weather-bound one week. Owing to landing at wrong point equipment had to be much reduced. Attacked 0045 hours on 28.2.43. High concentration plant totally destroyed. All present. No fighting.'

Since Haugland had detached himself from the attack party two days before the raid, London had remained completely in the dark about the operation. By now they would be fearing the worst. The group arrived at Skrykken at 2000 hours and quickly set about planning their long march to the Swedish border. Haugland and Skinnarland had already been there and taken their share of rations. Skinnarland would take over as the Swallow W/T operator in the Rjukan area from Haugland, who would gather intelligence, make contact with resistance fighters and give training to new recruits. But first they would both go into hiding until the German searches were over.

Five of the Gunnerside party – Rønneberg, Idland, Kayser, Strømsheim and Storhaug – would make the 400-kilometre journey, which they figured would take around ten days, weather permitting. Haukelid and Kjelstrup were to stay on the Hardangervidda; Poulsson and Helberg were to head to Oslo before deciding on further action.

But as the party prepared to go their separate ways at Skrykken, there was no sign of Helberg, and they started to worry about him as the storm raged. The party heading for Sweden planned to ski for as much of the journey as they could. 'The party would be in uniform and, in the event of our meeting any resistance, we were to fight our way through', Rønneberg recalled. On reaching the border they would split into two groups and report themselves to the authorities as political refugees, having destroyed all their weapons and equipment beforehand. On the morning of 4 March Rønneberg, Idland, Kayser, Strømsheim and Storhaug bade farewell to the rest of the men and set out on their frozen odyssey.

The real adventure, they would discover, was only just beginning.

8

Escape to Victory

For ten days following the raid, the SOE chiefs in Baker Street and the government's highest political and military officials, including Churchill, had no idea whether it had been carried out successfully. As each day passed, fears for the saboteurs grew until finally, at 1155 hours on 10 March, there was a crackle on the receiving set at one of SOE's country mansion signals stations in the shires. Haugland and Skinnarland had been unable to find the message, which Gunnerside said they would leave at Slettedal. It was only when Haukelid and Kjelstrup turned up that they heard the good news. The new arrivals cranked up the accumulator to generate plenty of power and erected the aerial on its bamboo mast as Haugland settled down to his keys. The message read as follows: 'Operation carried out with 100 percent success. High Concentration plant completely destroyed. Shots not exchanged since the Germans did not realise anything. The Germans do not appear to know whence they came or whither the party disappeared.' The historic message from Swallow caused jubilation in Downing Street, Whitehall and the headquarters of SOE.

Hitler's atomic bomb programme had been dealt a major blow. For how long was another matter, but for the time being at least the Allies could breathe a sigh of relief and raise a glass in the direction of Norway. The war in the west had already begun to swing to their advantage, but now the single most potent threat to their hopes of triumph had been eliminated.

Norway's notorious Reichskommissar Josef Terboven and General von Falkenhorst, the two most powerful Germans in the country, personally oversaw the massive search for the saboteurs over the coming weeks. The senior officer at the Vemork guard-house, along with several others, was removed from his post and banished to the Eastern Front as punishment.

At the same time, immediate and urgent measures were taken to rebuild the destroyed heavy water apparatus and reinforce the area's defence against future attacks. To the amusement of the locals, wanted posters were put up in the area offering rewards for information about 'tall, strongly-built young men with fair hair and blue eyes speaking Norwegian'. The description, of course, could apply to half of Norway's male population.

Kristiansen, the reindeer hunter whom the saboteurs had released, had blown their cover under interrogation by the Norwegian police. He had handed the English chocolate to local children; some of the wrappers were discovered and he was hauled in for questioning. Owing more to stupidity than malice (though no one knows for sure), he told his interrogators that his captors had been British soldiers. According to Helberg's account the hunter was confused by the Norwegian accents of those who had spoken to him and thought they were English. This was not as daft as it sounds. In Norway there are two of-ficial languages – Bokmål and Nynorsk – and hundreds of spoken dialects.

In the frantic search for information about the raid, wild rumours abounded that there were up to 2,000 British paratroopers in the mountains waiting to launch a full-scale attack, and a whole division was sent out to confront them. Figures of troops involved vary wildly, but at an absolute minimum there were about 2,000 at the height of the searches. Two hundred Norwegian Nazis from Quisling's NS party also joined the sweeps.

When the raiding party separated on 4 March, the Gunnerside group headed north at the start of their long trek to Sweden, Haukelid headed to the west side of the Hardanger plateau, while Kjelstrup also headed west to Vinje, where he planned to continue covert work. When the two of them finally emerged from their hideaways they would train detachments of local resistance fighters for the eventual overthrow of the Germans.

Helberg and Poulsson headed east to Oslo, going their own separate ways with a view to returning to Rjukan once the fall-out from the sabotage had settled. From there they would head to Notodden, a town about halfway between Oslo and Rjukan, where they would make contact with the resistance movement Milorg.

Poulsson made his way to the capital without major incident, spending the nights in a railway depot and a charcoal burner's hut before taking the train to Krødsherad on 8 March. The following day he met Helberg at an Oslo café as arranged. 'I have seldom been more pleased to see a human being,' recalled Poulsson, who, like the others, had feared his colleague might have perished in the storm or been captured. Helberg recalled: 'I had set out to meet up with the others when the storm broke and it began to blow very, very heavily. My map was blown away by a gust and after an hour of trying to find my way without one, I decided it was impossible in the weather and took refuge in a hut.'

When the razzia began, Haugland, the W/T operator, and Skinnarland took their belongings from the hut and camped in a tent in the mountains above Møsvatn lake. Using his binoculars Haugland watched the German troops scouring the valley. 'One time we were lying in a small tent on the highest mountain when we saw the German patrols below us and the planes above us. So we dug ourselves into the snow and created a living area with two rooms. We stayed there for several days and felt very safe. The Germans rarely came more than a day's march into the mountains because they were scared of having to spend the night up there.'

The troops searched every hut they could find on their maps as well as any others they came across. Often they would loot the huts, taking wineglasses and other goods and packing them on to horse-drawn sledges. Among the Germans were small parties from the Norwegian pro-Nazi Kongsvinger Battalion and a small group of pro-Nazi state policemen. (Some of the police were 'true' Norwegians who infiltrated the organisation to pass on vital information about German plans and operational activities.)

A Norwegian outdoorsman can look at a ski track and tell whether it is ten minutes, three hours or five days old, but the Germans didn't appear even to be looking for the most obvious clues. Part of the problem was that so many soldiers were deployed that they ended up creating an enormous and bewildering maze of tracks, making it even more difficult to find the fugitives.

Haukelid, who was also observing the searches from high up in the mountains, was astounded by the incompetence of the Germans. 'There is only one way to find people in the wilderness, not just in Norway but anywhere in the world – you have to hunt them in the same way in which they live,' he said.

On 20 April, an SOE operative in Oslo, code-named Parrott, wired the following message to London: 'Some German wounded soldiers arrived Oslo from closed Hardangervidda area. Reports say they were wounded in fights between various German patrols who met in mountains believing others were partisans. German SS patrols still searching closed area burning down all uninhabited mountain cottages. Norwegians living in Hardangervidda are under incessant supervision and forbidden to leave homes.'

One report said that no fewer than eighteen German soldiers were wounded in the firefights and were brought down by ambulance from the Hardanger 'highlands' to a hospital in Rjukan. A state of martial law was declared in the region and nobody was allowed to enter or leave without police permission. These were tough times for a local population already feeling the severe strain of occupation and deprivation. The lack of proper food was becoming a major problem, especially during the winter months when resistance was low and it was impossible to grow anything of their own and eat off the land. One resistance man reported that by the end of the 1942–43 winter in Rjukan, a town of no more than 5,500 people, there was one funeral per week. When the agent left the town, he had had no fat of any description for three weeks, and reported that during the razzia all the milk was commandeered by the Germans and even very young children were forced to go without.

One of the modern Grouse team – his clothing and equipment is as close as possible to the 1943 outfit.

When the original saboteurs landed they were carrying much more equipment.

Tracks of a reindeer herd on the Hardangervidda. A sight like this would have gladdened the hearts of the saboteurs in the winter of 1942–43.

We found the hut at Svensbu in remarkably good condition and (*below*) the Royal Marines and Norwegian soldiers who made up the modern 'Grouse' team. The interior is almost exactly the same as it would have been in 1942, except the walls would have been lined with reindeer hides.

The Valley at Rjukan and a view of the road to the plant. These photographs were taken from where the saboteurs rested on the railway line before the attack. Their approach was from left to right accross the hillside in the background and the Hardangervidda beyond.

The hut at Skyrkken – a very isolated place to stay even to-day – this is where Helberg's epic ski chase began

Members of Grouse at the 60th anniversary of the raid: (*left to right*) Jens Anton Poulsson, Klaus Helberg, Berger Strømsheim, Joachim Rønneberg, Knut Haugland. Helberg died a few days after this picture was taken.

F47/4   ·   **113**

Reference attached.   I have already discussed
the case with the Military Secretary, and he has
agreed that in this special case it would be most
invidious to try and distinguish between the degrees
of courage and fortitude displayed by these men.

He has therefore further agreed that each man
should be put in for an award, the leader for a D.S.O.,
the remaining officers for an M.C. and the men for
a Military Medal each.   He has asked me to send him
the citation direct and personally, and he will see
it through himself.   SN is now preparing it, and
I will get the approval of the Appointments and
Awards Committee before forwarding it to the Military
Secretary.

S.o. I think this is   M/
the proper procedure unless
you wish to forward the recommendations
straight to the P.M. which would be irregular   C.D.
                                                15.4.

The men of Operation Swallow/Gunnerside received military honours for their
bravery, as outlined in this War Office telegram.

The memorial outside the Vemork plant. The inscription reads:
'The Heavy Water sabotage at Vemork 28 February 1943' and includes
the names of all those involved in the raid.

'Before leaving we had to plan the route of our long retreat, which could be as long as six hundred kilometres,' said Rønneberg.

We obviously couldn't just draw a straight line from Rjukan to the Swedish border because that would take us through the populated areas of eastern Norway. So we had to go farther north, but we couldn't go south because there was a huge lake there which we would not be able to cross. We also worked out that we would have to go a long way north of Lillehammer because that's where the Germans had their skiing training, before turning back to the south-east towards Sweden.

SOE produced us three sets of maps in 1:100,000 scale, each of which contained twenty-six smaller, more detailed maps. One set we had pinned to the walls of the huts we stayed in before setting out and, having drawn a line of our intended route, each member of the withdrawal party was encouraged to study them so he had a good idea in his mind where we would be going.

When we set out from the depot, we anticipated it would take us ten days to reach Sweden. We had planned to march by night and sleep by day, but soon realised it was quicker and easier to do it the other way around.

The weather and snow conditions were first rate when the Gunnerside withdrawal party left Skrykken for Sweden, but they were soon struggling. Already weighed down by their poorly designed rucksacks, the five of them also had to haul a heavily laden toboggan, which was fine over hard snow but back-breaking when they ran into softer, wetter drifts, and even more gruelling when they came upon scrub and brushwood. It was, the usually uncomplaining Rønneberg recorded, 'an awful labour'. The first night they spent at an abandoned, isolated guest house called the Sterhotel, where they found some basic foodstuffs which allowed them to preserve their dwindling rations.

With the weather holding fine the following day, they set out on another exhausting leg of the journey, all the time going to great lengths to ensure that they would not be spotted by the enemy. Two scouts went out ahead of the other three and scoured the horizons with binoculars before they all proceeded. After making good progress in the morning, the afternoon brought with it a desperate physical battle as they laboured to transport the cumbersome toboggan down a steep, rugged slope and then drag it up an equally challenging ascent on the other side.

The entire party was shattered by the time they stumbled across a hunting lodge next to Lake Rødungen. Rønneberg had developed a painful inflammation of the hand which made his progress all the more difficult, while the terrain, a mesmerising mass of white peaks, valleys and lakes, made orientation difficult. Over the following few days, they were forced to rely on the compass for directions as they were unable to work out their route from the maps.

March 7 was a Sunday, a day when many Norwegians came out to ski, and, fearing they might be spotted, they decided to lie low until the morning. There was a moment of panic when they saw a lone skier approaching the hut. Quickly, they piled all their equipment into a back room and blacked out the windows, then locked the door and hid. The man went into the hut next door and the party were forced to lie on the floor for over an hour before he took his leave and disappeared into the distance.

The following day they waited till the light was fading before setting out across the great expanse of the Hallingdalen valley, where they could be easily sighted from every direction. Once they were across, a spider's web of different paths and tracks left them completely confused, and they were forced to bed down in the snow in their sleeping bags, wet through from an earlier river crossing.

At first light they decided to postpone breakfast and, after managing to find their bearings, headed for a hut about one hour's hard march away, where they could dry out their clothes and equipment. By now the wind had picked up considerably and the temperature had plunged to well below zero. Despite the conditions they decided to press on, knowing that every stride took them farther away from the razzia that had fanned out from the plant at Vemork. By the evening they had reached a place called Fjellstølen, about 20 kilometres west of Aurdalsfjord, where, to their joy, they found a surprisingly comfortable but unoccupied farmhouse, stocked with flour and bannock bread.

On the sixth day of the march they were taken by surprise when they passed two men on the way up a mountainside. The Gunnerside party were dressed entirely in white, and their machine guns were poking out of the top of their rucksacks. The two groups waved to each other as they passed, the two men assuming that the party were German troops on exercise. At 2000 hours they reached Aurdalsfjord and were disturbed to discover that much of the ice covering had melted. They found a point on the southern shore where the ice appeared still to stretch right the way across. Rønneberg took it upon himself to test its strength before ordering the others across. Crawling on all fours and using an axe to test the ice in front, he slowly made his way to the other side as the others watched nervously from the bank. It was weak, but just about passable, Rønneberg thought, and the others tentatively followed him across, each man keeping a good distance between himself and the next. By midnight they had climbed almost 1,000 metres above sea level before breaking into a hut owned, it turned out, by an engineer called Christiansen, who they discovered to their delight was a fervent patriot. The walls were covered with pictures of the King of Norway, Haakon VII, as well as reproductions of the true Norwegian constitution.

The following day, the weather took a turn for the worse. Heavy cloud blotted out the sky and the temperature rose sharply, making the snow 'warm' and wet and very hard going for skiers. During their stop for lunch, they felt the first depressing drops of rain on their heads. By the end of the day they had virtually ground to a standstill in the soggy conditions, which pushed them to the point of exhaustion.

Their equipment, too, was being tested to the limit of its capabilities. Overall, the party were satisfied with the kit they had been issued, particularly the woollen British battledress they wore throughout the retreat. But they found the shirts too hot and took to keeping them in their rucksacks until the evenings, when they wore them next to the skin as their underwear had become soaked by sweat and damp. Their string vests were excellent for warmth and helped their outer clothes dry much faster, but those with more sensitive skin developed sores from them. Likewise, their rabbit-skin jockstraps provided excellent protection against the cold, but would chafe the skin when the men began to sweat and became particularly irritating during hard skiing. Some found the jockstraps too hot if the temperatures were higher than minus 15 Centigrade. But the greatest bugbear was the rucksack, with its poor design and thin, pain-inducing straps, which bit into the shoulders.

Over the next few days the temperature dropped again and the party made good progress, but their supplies were rapidly running out, decreasing in inverse proportion to the amount of energy they were expending as they slogged their way through this forbidding wilderness. Idland found the going particularly difficult as he was the least experienced skier, but his great determination drove him on – he didn't want to hold the party back. The team had a ritual which helped keep up their spirits during the march. 'We had twenty-six maps to guide us out of Norway and every time we had finished with one we had the great pleasure of burning it, knowing that we were getting ever closer to our destination,' recalled Rønneberg.

On 13 March, the tenth day of their withdrawal, they spotted two German planes, Junker 52s, but they did not appear to be searching the area below and they thought they were probably post planes, heading from Oslo to Trondheim, because they were following the established route along Gudbrandsalen. The next two nights they had to spend outside in their sleeping bags, having been unable to find a suitably isolated hut. The food situation was becoming critical, and they were forced to divert from their route to break into huts to search for supplies. Often they were disappointed, but they found just enough flour and bannock bread to keep body and soul together for a while longer.

Their journey had reached a critical point. They were not far from the Swedish border, but they were weary and hungry and needed to be more alert than ever as there were several German detachments as well as Norwegian Nazis operating in the area, trying to prevent refugees – and resistance fighters – reaching the border. The plan was to cross the River Glomma close to the town of Rena, but Storhaug, who was from the area, mistakenly led the party six kilometres out of their way. They were completely lost in the complex network of hills and valleys and unable to work out where they were from the maps. Orientation was easier when they were high in the mountains because they were able to see the lie of the land and use their maps. The problems came when they were in the lowlands and had no natural points of reference to guide them and were forced to use their compasses.

'In these situations you come to depend on each other and it is important not to get irritated,' said Rønneberg. 'It is very easy to get annoyed by small details or other people's habits, but if you lose your temper you can destroy the atmosphere in the group. So in those circumstances, I felt it was best you get up and walk away until you calmed down.'

Eventually they managed to find the river, but to their despair it was entirely free of ice. The party had no idea about the strength of German troops in the area, and after they had taken shelter close to the river it was decided that Storhaug would have to make contact with a local man he knew to be a 'true' Norwegian. Four hours later he returned with a stolen boat, and the party made a hasty crossing of the river before darting into the wooded mountains on the other side. For the next two nights they were forced to sleep out in the open again, their clothes and sleeping bags wet through. Snow, as the Norwegians say, is a great blanket but a poor mattress. Nobody managed to sleep on account of the cold and their hunger. 'The lack of food had the effect of making one dream all day of groaning tables, loaded with food,' Rønneberg recorded. The party were tantalisingly close to the border but the final kilometres were especially hard going. 'It was dreadful broken and stony country, through scrub and thick woods, with no visibility,' Rønneberg added.

Finally, at 2015 hours on 18 March, fifteen days after they set out from Skrykken, exhausted, starving but elated after their 400-kilometre trek, they set foot on the neutral soil of Sweden. They all shook hands, congratulated each other and treated themselves to their first open fire since their return to Scandinavia. According to Rønneberg, 'for the last night as British soldiers we climbed into our sleeping bags, our faithful weapons beside us. We all had a splendid night.' The following morning, after finishing the final scraps of their rations, the five of them dug a hole and buried most of their equipment and went to great trouble to make sure they had nothing British left in their possession. They changed into civilian outdoor clothing: thick stockings, jumper and wind-proof suit. In their rucksacks they carried a little ski wax, spare socks, a cup and spoon, a sleeping bag, half a block of pemmican and a little Norwegian money.

Their first priority was to find food. The lack of nutrition over the past two weeks had left them in a very weak condition, vulnerable to illness. They also needed a cover story to tell the Swedish authorities so that they could be classified as political refugees and given free passage into the country. The story was as follows: they were unknown to each other before they were sent to a German work camp at a place called Dombås, where they had been put to work building barracks and storehouses. They had escaped and formed a resistance cell, performing illegal activities, but, fearing for their lives, they had fled to Sweden. In order to ensure that they described the work camp in the same way, they decided to use their training base in Scotland as the model.

They walked for 20 kilometres before they were picked up by

a Swedish patrol and taken to the local sheriff's house. They were treated warmly by the Swedes and placed in a hospital where they were deloused, washed and their clothes disinfected and dried. That night they ate out in a hotel restaurant, relishing their first proper meal since they had left England over a month earlier. The following day they were all interrogated, and despite the suspicion aroused by the fact that all their clothes were almost exactly the same, the Swedish police happily accepted their cover story. They were granted leave to travel, without guards, first to Kjeseter and then to Stockholm, where they reported to the British legation, which gave them money and ration cards to tide them over until they could book their boat journey to the United Kingdom. A telegram was sent by SOE in Stockholm to London, reporting the safe arrival of the men.

'As soon as we made contact with the British legation, the Swedish were happy to get us off their hands,' said Rønneberg. 'The British gave us ration cards and money and we went shopping to buy outdoor equipment we knew we could not get back in Britain, such as special cooking equipment, Silva compasses, watches, winter boots and ski shoes.'

The success of their escape earned praise from their masters at SOE. 'The difficulties of this march in winter conditions with the added strain of short rations and hard lying make it a most noteworthy achievement,' the first official reaction soberly recorded.

At the end of the month they set sail from Bromma across the North Sea, and thirty hours later they reached British shores. The final leg of the journey was by far the most relaxing of the past six weeks as they headed to London by train, happy to be alive and to be able to report the successful execution of one the war's most spectacular sabotage acts. Rønneberg remembers:

On our arrival we were handed a cup of tea. It was a strange feeling because here I was back in Britain, but I felt like I was at home. We often used to refer to it as home when we were in Norway, and when I look back on the war I will never forget the welcome that the British showed us. If you were out in a dancing hall or in a pub, people were always very friendly. Most knew about the Norwegian situation and they also knew about the actions of the Norwegian merchant navy bringing supplies to their country, and they were very appreciative. We never felt like guests in Britain, more like partners in the same cause. Since the war I always felt I have had two homelands: one where I was born and one where I lived during the war.

While delighted with the success of the operation and the ensuing escape, Colonel Wilson at SOE was alarmed that some of those privy to it had failed to preserve the utmost secrecy it had been accorded. Never was the term 'heavy water' to be used, even in inter-departmental communiqués, but this had been forgotten in some of the messages being passed to and fro. 'I am most disturbed to read of what has been said under the heading of Norway in regard to the Gunnerside operation,' Wilson wrote in a memo to the War Office. 'I feel that a grave breach of security is involved. The term "heavy water" is covered by the code name "Lurgan" ... Every effort has been made to prevent a leakage of information that the recent sabotage at the Norsk Hydro Works was connected with anything more than the stoppage of the supply of nitrogen fertilisers. If there is any way in which this particular reference can be struck off the records, I shall be glad if you will put it into force at once.'

The problem was that the success of the raid had attracted great attention in the press and Wilson's calls for secrecy were rather a case of shutting the gate after the horse had bolted. *The Times* correspondent in Stockholm had filed a report about the raid on 15 March, using the term 'heavy water', but to his credit and the government's relief he had gone into no detail about the product's intended use, saying only that it was 'supposedly for the purposes of war industries'.

Wilson received a reply from the War Office saying that the circulation of details of the sabotage among political and military personnel was so limited that it did not matter whether the term 'heavy water' was used. It also pointed out that a number of newspapers had used the phrase in their reports of the action and that the Germans knew that the Allies knew what they were trying to do at Vemork. In other words, who are we trying to kid?

The story of Helberg's escape is almost worth a book in its own right. His colleagues said of him that he was a man with a great talent for getting out of trouble. Cool, resourceful, brave and quick witted, Helberg showed all these qualities in abundance to evade capture. The account of his escape, which he gave to his astonished commanders back in England later in 1943, reads like a chapter out of a James Bond novel. In passing on the report, Colonel Wilson wrote, 'the attached is an epic of cool headedness, bravery and resource'.

In early April Swallow reported to England that Helberg had been shot trying to escape the Germans. Tributes were paid by all who knew him at SOE and the Linge Company. Wilson led the marks of respect, describing Helberg as 'one of the most conscientious members of the Linge Company and in the most varying circumstances proved himself thoughtful and considerate'.

Directly after the raid, Helberg went to Oslo, where he met up with Poulsson and laid low for a few weeks, waiting for the German searches in the Rjukan region to run their course. Their original plan to head to the town of Notodden to recruit and train more resistance fighters was considered too dangerous during the clampdown by the Germans and the quisling security forces.

Helberg had specifically requested to stay in Norway, partly because he was 'known' to the Swedish authorities after spending two months in prison there, and partly because he wanted to move the Gunnerside/Swallow equipment dump to a safer place. Towards the end of March he was told by the resistance that it would be safe enough to return to the Hardangervidda to collect the cache, and he left Oslo on 22 March. Poulsson left for Sweden four days later with a view to returning to Britain for a short period. When Helberg arrived back in the Telemark region he was told by a contact that there were no Germans in the vicinity. In fact, the area, which had been designated 'restricted' the day before, was crawling with Germans.

Helberg spent his first night in a hut the saboteurs had broken into in the build-up to the operation. He slept for fourteen hours, deep into the following day. Shortly after he left, the hut was reduced to a smouldering pile of ashes as the search parties torched hut after hut in the district. On 25 March, still unaware of the huge German presence around the Hardangervidda, Helberg headed to the Jansbu hut at Skrykken, where the Gunnerside party had taken refuge from the blizzard after the parachute drop, and where they had been surprised by the reindeer hunter.

Gunnerside had left some arms and other equipment buried near by, and it was Helberg's task to fetch them. He opened the door to discover that the Germans had been there before him – the whole place had been ransacked. Immediately he ran outside, fearful that he was being watched, and as he opened the door he saw three Germans racing towards him on skis, about 100 metres away. The area around the hut is completely flat and featureless; the Germans must have been lying in wait. He quickly put on his skis and rucksack, placed his Colt .32 pistol in his pocket and set off south as fast as his skis could carry him. The Germans shouted at him to stop and then opened fire, the bullets whistling and thudding into the snow around him as he fled. 'I increased my pace so they had to stop shooting and then a first class long-distance ski race began,' recalled Helberg in his official report. 'I had a half year's training to my credit and was in splendid form.'

After about an hour, two of the Germans gave up the chase, but the third, an excellent skier and clearly very fit, continued to bear down on Helberg. 'He was a big, weather-beaten fellow in white camouflage costume and he seemed to be in terrific form,' said Helberg. He headed for the mountains and as directly into the bright sun as possible, so as to blind his pursuer if he decided to open fire again. After a while, he worked out that the German was quicker than him on the flat and the downhill, but he had the edge on him uphill. Unlike his pursuer Helberg was also carrying a rucksack and his skis were in a very poor condition and had not been properly waxed.

After about two hours, with the German gradually gaining on him, Helberg reached the top of a steep slope and realised that he would probably be caught if he attempted to descend it. With the sun low on the horizon, he stopped and decided to shoot it out as in an old-fashioned duel. The German shouted '*Hände hoch*!' (Hands up!) but was clearly surprised to see that Helberg was brandishing a Colt .32, a superior pistol to his own Luger. Helberg fired first. 'I realised that whoever emptied his magazine first would lose because at that distance nobody would have a realistic chance of hitting. So I stood there as a target,' recorded Helberg. He struggled to catch his breath as the German emptied his whole magazine. He missed with every shot, and when he heard the click of the empty handgun he turned and fled. Helberg pursued him for a short distance and when he was 20 metres away fired one shot. The German staggered, stopped and slumped over his ski sticks. Helberg had no idea whether he killed him or not.

His adventure, however, was only just beginning. To avoid leaving any trace of his movements, he decided to head down to the hard ice on the lakes and continue from there. The sun had by now long since set and he was enveloped in darkness. Unable to see more than a few yards ahead of him, he fell over a sheer precipice, and broke his left shoulder. 'The drop seemed very deep, possibly 40–50 metres,' he noted.

Happily, though, his skis remained intact, and he was able to continue, albeit in great pain. After lying out in the cold, buried under the snow for a couple of hours' rest, Helberg found a farm he knew at Lien, but his relief soon turned to alarm when he was told by the wife of his contact that there were fifty Hird policemen and Gestapo based at a neighbouring farm, no more than 300 metres away. Her husband had been roped into guiding them through the mountains in their search for the 'English' saboteurs. Helberg was exhausted after almost thirty-six hours on his skis and was also in considerable pain, but he continued to

Møsstrand, to another farm, before heading to a village called Rauland.

He was just a few kilometres short of his destination when he ran into a German patrol. Helberg might have panicked and fled but, keeping his cool, he produced his identity card and told the Germans that he had been out helping them with their search for the English. SOE had drummed into its 'students' the importance of having a good cover story. Never go anywhere without having a good reason to be there, they were told. Often it was just plain bad luck that a resistance fighter or secret agent was arrested, because periodically the Germans would make a mass sweep of an area and by the law of averages a number of agents would inevitably be among those rounded up. The Germans had introduced a number of schemes to try to control the Norwegians and restrict their movements around the country. People were not allowed to travel more than 30 kilometres from their home and everybody was issued with identity cards, zone cards and ration cards.

Helberg, as ever, was well prepared and remarkably cool. The documents he carried were perfect fakes, and after calmly telling the patrol that he was on their side he was allowed to proceed to the house he knew. When he got there he found it was full of German soldiers, but with the same bluff and bravado he won them over and spent the next two nights drinking and playing cards with them. One of them even bandaged his arm for him and arranged for him to see a German doctor.

The next day Helberg found himself even deeper in the lions' den, surrounded by the people he was most trying to avoid. He was driven in a German Red Cross car to the town of Dalen, from where he could catch a boat then a train to Oslo in order to get proper hospital treatment. He was to present himself at the Bandaksli Hotel, where he would be examined by a doctor and granted permission to continue his journey.

'I had not eaten well for a long time and I remember having a very good trout dinner and going to bed feeling very happy with myself,' recalled Helberg.

He had just got into bed when he heard a great commotion downstairs, with orders being barked in German. Helberg feared the worst. It looked as if his number was finally up. But he kept his cool once again and decided against trying to run for it. It turned out that the Germans were not carrying out a search after all. Terboven, Norway's Reichskommissar, had arrived with his entourage of senior ranking officers. He was in the area over-seeing the razzia and most of the hotel guests were turned out of their rooms to accommodate the new arrivals. Many were forced to spend the night sitting in the living areas downstairs, but Helberg, for some reason, was allowed to stay in his room, which turned out to be next door to Terboven. All he wanted to do was escape, but all the doors were barred by SS officers and others were on guard outside.

At dinner that night an attractive young woman had refused to succumb to Terboven's dubious charms and declined his invi-tation to join his party over dinner. She told him that her father was a colonel in the Royal Norwegian Army, now in England. Terboven was incensed by what he saw as the impertinence of the young girl. How dare she humiliate a man of his stature?

At five o'clock the following morning there was a knock at Helberg's door and a Gestapo officer ordered him to congregate with the other Norwegian guests in the sitting room. This was a highly anxious moment for Helberg, who stood out from the other guests like a beacon. He was the only single person in a group of couples and, unlike the others, he had a sunburnt face, which anyone with their wits about them would have known had been acquired from being out in the wilderness. They sat there in silence for five and a half hours before a Wehrmacht officer informed them that Terboven had been upset by the guests' behaviour and had ordered that all of them were to be sent to the concentration camp at Grini.

Women over fifty and very elderly men were allowed to stay, but seventeen of the group were herded on to a bus. Helberg, his pistol tucked into his holster, immediately began plotting his escape. (Some reports claim that Helberg's pistol fell out as he boarded the bus but he bluffed his way out of the situation. But Helberg himself makes no mention of this in his official report.) There was only one door, right at the front by the driver, and an SS guard sat in the seat closest to it while three more SS men on motorbikes with sidecars escorted the bus. The passengers were told that they would be shot if they tried to escape. They set off at around midday, and Helberg knew that they would not reach Grini in daylight because it was a slow bus and the roads were in a poor condition. His only chance of escape would come after nightfall, when the right-hand side of the bus, where the door was located, came alongside a wooded area with a downward slope.

Helberg sat next to the attractive girl whose defiance had provoked Terboven, and they struck up a lively, jovial conversation. Helberg was deliberately trying to attract the interest of the SS soldier at the front, and sure enough the German eventually made his way to the back of the bus. The SS man ('a nice fellow', according to Helberg) joined in the conversation and, clearly enamoured of the girl, suggested that he and Helberg swap seats, saying a man with a broken arm should have more room for his comfort. Helberg was only too happy to oblige him. As the bus climbed the hill, Helberg waited for his chance to jump, but for most of the way the adjacent ground sloped upwards, making it impossible for him to make a clean getaway.

Time was running out, but finally Helberg saw his chance and leapt from the speeding bus. He landed heavily, further damaging his shoulder and also his head. The bus and motorcycles screeched to a halt. He ran into the woods, chased by the Germans, but the snow was thick and he crashed into a high fence which he could not pass. A stick grenade exploded about five yards from him and he hurtled back towards the bus and sprinted across the road. Two more grenades were thrown at him, the first exploding harmlessly some distance away. The second, though, hit him square between the shoulders but failed to go off. 'I think that the German had thrown the hand grenade in haste because about four seconds later there was an explosion,' he recalled. Helberg raced into the dark woods, where he hid. The Germans fired a volley of shots into the darkness, but then gave up the search, presumably in the belief that Helberg would freeze to death or had been killed by a bullet. It was these shots in the dark which led to a report reaching Swallow and Milorg that Helberg had been killed as he fled.

His arm was aching, it was raining heavily and he was ravenously hungry. Unable to return to the road or stay out in the woods, Helberg took refuge in a lunatic asylum at a place called Lier, where he had heard that the staff were 'true' Norwegians. He knocked on the door of an outbuilding at one o'clock in the morning. His arm was swollen, his face cut, his clothes filthy and his trousers torn. Inside, there were two men and two women holding some kind of drinking party and, just as he had suspected and hoped, they took him in without any questions being asked before giving him food and clean clothes. The following day one of the doctors called for an ambulance and he was taken to a hospital in nearby Drammen, where he stayed for eighteen days before being released.

The Germans made no attempt to launch a man hunt for Helberg after his escape. In all likelihood, the German troopers told their officers that they had killed him, so as to avoid being punished for letting him escape. Reports of his death had reached the local Norwegian resistance group, and when he made contact with them in a town called Asker nobody believed his story. Although he did not know it at the time he was suspected of being an 'agent provocateur' and was held by his compatriots for four weeks as they tried to establish his identity. The delay began to irritate Helberg, and he told his 'hosts' that he was going to leave for Oslo despite their threats to have him 'court-martialled'.

One of the several 'export' organisations operating in Oslo arranged for his passage to the Swedish border. Before leaving he made contact with Haugland, who was delighted to discover that reports of his friend's death had proved to be entirely groundless. On 25 May Wilson at SOE was given the uplifting news. 'This has a very important bearing on the Gunnerside operation since it seems that the enemy are still unaware as to how it was carried out. This explains, too, why the search on the Hardangervidda was carried out for such a lengthy period of time,' Wilson recorded.

Sweden was neutral territory, but many Norwegians suspected the Swedes of being largely pro-Nazi, especially at the start of the war. All the roads into Sweden were guarded, but the Norwegian resistance fighters simply walked in over the mountains and through the forests before heading for Stockholm. And it was thus that Helberg completed the last leg of his incredible escape before boarding a plane for the UK on 2 June after three months on the run.

Haugland's first task after the razzia had petered out was to bring Skinnarland up to speed as a W/T operator. The brevity of Skinnarland's training left him a little short of quality as an operator, and at the outset he filed a number of what the FANYs back in London called 'indecipherables'. But under Haugland's expert guidance he soon became highly proficient.

> He [Skinnarland] was a long way below the required standard so we headed up to a remote hut high in the mountains where we knew we would be safe and then set about training. I built an improvised radio set with some materials I had and began sending messages to Einar. We used the stories from old magazines we found in the hut to send messages back and forth. He got faster and faster as well as more accurate and after about a month or so I got him up to the right level. After I had finished training Einar and the German patrols had disappeared from the area, I thought it was safe to head down from the mountains. The first thing I did was go to a farm and have my first bath in about five months.
>
> I went to Notodden to train some recruits and I was surprised to discover that my brother was head of the underground organisation there.

(His brother was later caught and after being tortured under interrogation he was sent to a concentration camp in Poland.)

Haugland gave training not just in W/T communications, his area of great expertise, but also in the use of guns and explosives. He conducted similar training exercises in Kongsberg and Oslo before slipping across the border to Sweden and returning to England. While in Oslo, Haugland discovered that the German D/F (Direction/Finding) operations were far more sophisticated and active than they had been up near Rjukan.

These signals tracking units could be mounted on trucks or aircraft to sniff out covert operators. They were highly accurate, and within minutes the Germans were able to establish the location of the transmitter. The more time spent on air, the more likely it was that the operators would be pinpointed, captured, interrogated and either sent to a concentration camp or executed. In urban areas the operators had to be constantly on the move to dodge their trackers, but this was particularly difficult in the first years of the war when the bulk of the transmission sets made it difficult to carry them around without attracting attention. As the war progressed the Allies developed lighter, better versions built into small leather cases, and the operators themselves developed ingenious ways of hiding their equipment. Lavatories, whose cisterns had been specially adapted, were a favourite place, often with the aerial of the transmitter running down inside the flushing chain. One Norwegian operator even kept his equipment in a cage holding a fox in his back garden.

While he was on the Hardangervidda, Haugland was fortunate not to have to take such extreme measures to conceal his position or equipment. There were no roads on the plateau and, curiously, the Germans rarely used aeroplanes because they thought the operator would be based in Rjukan or an outlying village. Haugland knew this and much more because one of his contacts talked every day to the Germans in charge of the D/F station in the Telemark region. In Oslo, the Germans were far more efficient, using mobile vans that could detect communications up to three kilometres away.

By the end of the war the Allied secret services had 200 operators embedded throughout Norway, but it took a long time to establish the network and there was a good deal of recrimination and finger-pointing in Norway and back in Britain before it began to operate smoothly. At the British end, there appeared to be a lot of bureaucratic dragging of feet, but in Norway it was ham-fisted typing by ill-trained or incompetent operators causing the headaches.

An SOE communiqué from Stockholm to HQ in London spells out the frustrations felt by some Norwegian operators. It is not clear whether the author is referring to all the operators in Norway or just some in a particular region, but the language is unusually strong.

> It is clear from the tone of communications ... that they are exasperated to the last degree at the continued failure to get things going in spite of the efforts made at their end, and with all respect, it seems to us that the communications section in the UK are anything but helpful, and it is hardly to be wondered at if they are fretful ... I would venture to ask that the various stations are dealt with as promptly as possible, as it is obviously disheartening for those in Norway who have done all this preparatory work to have to wait for weeks, if not months, before any decision is taken.

There was also considerable incompetence at the Norwegian end
as operators struggled to send decipherable telegrams, or even
make contact. In his official report after returning to Britain via
Sweden in mid-August 1943, Haugland, who had spent months
trying to train up from scratch or improve existing operators,
professed astonishment at the delays, misunderstandings and
general muddle, as well as the excuses for failure being offered.
'My station was tried in all kinds of weather and terrain, often
between high mountains, but we always managed to get through.
Ninety-two telegrams were sent and approximately fifty received.
Only once was I presented with an undecipherable telegram – a
mistake which was soon put right.'

After a time, Haukelid and Kjelstrup felt it safe to make contact
with the two W/T operators and afterwards the two of them,
together with Skinnarland, headed to the Svensbu hut, which had
been ransacked by the Germans. They found the hidden cache of
equipment nearby and reburied it miles away as a precaution
before Skinnarland rejoined Haugland and Haukelid teamed up
again with Kjelstrup. The latter pair stayed up in the mountains
for much of the spring and summer in a hut they built called
Bamsebu, from where they established an intelligence and resistance network.

Living off a diet of red meat slowly took its toll on Kjelstrup's
health and he began to suffer from a form of beriberi owing to the
nutritional deficiencies in his dietary regime. In the autumn it was
decided that he should return to the UK to recover his strength.
(Poulsson, the Grouse/Swallow leader, was the first to return to
Britain after a decision was taken that there was little he could do
for the time being and his presence would only compromise others.)

As spring melted the snow, Haukelid and Kjelstrup knew that the warm weather would lead to an influx of walkers and fishermen on to the Hardangervidda. Fearing their position could be compromised, they decided to head to Oslo for a period, before returning to the Hardangervidda. On the way to the capital Kjelstrup fell through some ice and Haukelid had to scramble to save him. The commotion alerted the residents of a local hamlet on the lakeside, who rushed out to help the strangers. They were taken to a farmer's house, where Kjelstrup was given warm food and dried out his clothes. The locals stood around staring at them as if they were aliens, and as soon as they were ready they set off again on their journey before any quisling among them could alert the authorities.

While in Oslo, Haukelid had stayed at a friend of his family's. One day his father came to the door. Haukelid had not seen him for almost two years, but following the strictest rules of his training he hid while his father came in and chatted with their friends. Haukelid was desperate to reveal himself and tell his father he was safe and well, but to do so would endanger both him and his father. The Germans had the most persuasive means of extracting information from their captives and Haukelid could not bear the idea of his father being brutalised as a result of his own sentimental weakness. So he just bit his lip.

That was the last time Haukelid had news of his father. Later in the war he learned that he had died in Grini concentration camp after the Gestapo had found a cache of W/T sets hidden by the resistance on his property.

9

Ferry of Death

The heavy water stocks and the apparatus needed for its production were completely destroyed in the raid, but predictions that it would put the operation out of action for over a year or longer soon proved to be over-optimistic. The Germans ordered that the plant was to be rebuilt and returned to full capacity within two months. Great efforts and resources were channelled into repairing the damage and resuming production. The good Norwegians inside the plant could do their best to cause some delay to the reconstruction, but they risked severe punishment if they were suspected of deliberately hampering the process.

Through Skinnarland, SOE received various estimates of the time it would take for the Germans to restart production and rejoin the race to build the world's first atomic bomb. One intelligence report suggested that production had started again by the end of May after the Germans took heavy water apparatus destined for a new plant at nearby Såheim and simply installed it at Vemork instead. Other sources suggested that the programme would not be restarted until the early autumn.

In July, Skinnarland cabled London to tell them that production of heavy water would return to full capacity in mid-August. Skinnarland's information was seen as the most reliable, as he was known to have good contacts inside the plant. Amid this fog of information during the months following the raid, the Allies set about making fresh plans to attack the plant again. Every option was placed on the table, including carpet-bombing the complex, blowing dams or finding an employee at the plant willing to destroy it before giving himself up to avoid widespread reprisals. The latter was effectively a suicide mission, but the planners were confident that someone there would be prepared to lay down their life for the wider cause of defeating Nazism. 'It may well be that there are men, with local knowledge, willing to take the job on, even under such a condition,' Professor Tronstad told his colleagues.

Meanwhile Tronstad was baffled by the Germans' persistence with their 'utilisation' method of production, when a new 'combustion' method, familiar to most scientists in the field by then, would mean a dramatic increase in production. Tronstad found it difficult to believe that German scientists, world leaders in this area up to the start of the war, had not ordered a switch of methods. The professor warned his colleagues at SOE to be on their guard for intelligence that the Germans were indeed about to change tack. This, he said, should be regarded as 'an alarm signal'. Tronstad put forward a number of proposals for a second attack on Vemork, including the blowing of a dam called Skarfoss, which would put the plant out of action without endangering the lives of the people in the valley in the way that the destruction of the Møsvatn dam certainly would have.

The sabotage act in February led to major strengthening of German defences at Vemork, making a *coup de main* attack virtually impossible. Sappers immediately set about erecting dozens of barbed-wire barriers and minefields, the strengths of the garrisons were increased, all doors to the main building bar one were bricked up, while the windows on the ground floor were given iron-mesh fronts to prevent bombs being thrown through them.

A huge force would be needed to carry out a direct ground assault on the plant, but there was little prospect of so many being able to effect a successful escape over 400 kilometres to Sweden. SOE began to talk openly about a massive bombing raid, something previously considered to be out of the question for moral and political reasons. The United States Air Force (USAAF) had shown in other theatres of the war that relatively precise bombing was possible. But 'relative' was no good if you happened to live within a few hundred yards of Vemork, and the Norwegian government would almost certainly quash any proposal on the grounds that such a raid risked the lives of dozens of innocent Norwegians and was also likely to result in the annihilation of the economically vital industrial plant.

The principal purpose of the Norsk Hydro plant was the production of nitrates for civilian use. Fertilisers for agriculture made up roughly 95 per cent of the plant's output. The remaining 5 per cent consisted of technical products like nitrate acid, ammonia and soda, while the 'heavy water' was a by-product. Before the war, most of the fertiliser was sold for Norwegian and Scandinavian use, but once the outbreak of war had closed Norway's markets to the outside world production went entirely to Scandinavian clients. In the year up to the end of June 1943 the plant produced 85,000 tons of fertilisers, of which a quarter stayed in Norway and the rest was divided among the other three Scandinavian countries.

Norsk Hydro's production was important not just to the economy but also to the survival of thousands of people suffering severe food shortages in the occupied territories. The Allies' blockade of Germany had prevented any imports of food and other supplies reaching northern Europe. Norway had always depended heavily on the import of food, but since the war the inhabitants had been forced to try to eke out a living from the very limited natural resources of their own land. Owing to the harsh climate, there are no permanent crops in Norway, and only 3 per cent of the land is arable. Germany's banning of commercial fishing to crack down on the traffic of resistance fighters to and from the UK compounded the food crisis. Against this background, it is not difficult to understand Norwegian hostility to the destruction of their fertiliser stocks.

An SOE memorandum dated 20 August 1943 suggested that the bombing option should be given active consideration by the chiefs of staff, but that the Norwegian High Command and government should, for the time being, be kept in the dark about any such plans. But as the war was beginning to swing the Allies' way, SOE also began to muse on the wisdom of protecting rather than destroying the plant in the event of a withdrawal of German forces to bolster their strength elsewhere in the European theatre.

The February raid was a stunning success and a welcome boon for SOE, whose activities and success rate had been the subject of some criticism from a number of quarters, not least from the intelligence service SIS, which felt that SOE's actions compromised their purely intelligence-gathering agents in the field. There was also ongoing tension with Milorg, the Norwegian resistance movement, which complained that SOE operations continued to jeopardise their members as they often triggered reprisals in the form of mass arrests and increased searches. The Norwegian government was another party that viewed SOE's operations with suspicion for the same reasons. SOE needed a spectacular success to justify their existence. The Vemork raid gave it to them.

A letter from Major Rheam at SOE's training department to Colonel Wilson at the Norwegian section spelt out the feelings of pride engendered by the actions of the Vemork saboteurs. 'I think Gunnerside was a most magnificent show and I have suggested to Colonel Woolrych that some "secure" version of the story should be told to all our students as an example for them to live up to.'

Rønneberg, meanwhile, had compiled a comprehensive report on the raid, attached to which is a handwritten message from a high-ranking Whitehall official or minister. It reads: 'A magnificent report of a great effort. Well planned and beautifully executed. If you return the report to me I will have a condensed edition made for the P.M.'

While plans to bomb the plant in a major daylight raid began to attract support in military circles, major political problems were brewing. Hitler's atomic energy programme remained an issue of the highest concern to the Allies, and both Churchill and Roosevelt continued to take an active interest in it. On 5 October an internal SOE memo stated: 'You will see that the "powers-that-be" wish us to consider whether we can have another go at the Vemork plant ... It is apparent that the view of the authorities is that we ought not to have regard to Norwegian post-war interests if these form an obstacle to the most effective plan.'

On 16 October, 1943 word from on high in Whitehall arrived at SOE and Combined Operations, ending all chance of a ground assault or sabotage raid on the Vemork plant. 'I regret to state that we have come to the conclusion that such an operation would not be practical politics at the moment,' read a letter from the War Cabinet Offices. 'As regards attack from the air, we quite realise that no low-level attack would be a practical proposition, but would there be no chance of a medium-level precision attack in daylight by United States aircraft? Although this would be a very difficult operation, it does seem to be the best chance of doing really conclusive damage.'

The problem, of course, was that there was really no such thing as 'precision' bombing as we know it today. The heavy water stocks were kept in the basement of a sturdily constructed seven-storey concrete building, and to ensure their destruction would involve the dropping of hundreds of tons of explosive, most of which was likely to fall in the surrounding area. The Norwegians simply would not agree to it, and if the Allies were to proceed regardless there would be serious political and diplomatic consequences to the inevitable bloodshed. However, the feeling at the highest political and military levels in the Allied establishment was that the deaths of innocent Norwegians and damage to the Norwegian economy were a lesser evil than the possible destruction of at least one entire city and the sudden defeat of the Allies that would inevitably follow production of a German atomic bomb. Unpleasant but a price worth paying – this seemed to be the general feeling.

One man who needed no encouragement to launch a devastating air strike on Vemork was Major Leslie Groves, the head of the US atomic bomb project 'Manhattan', who had demanded the destruction of any installation in occupied territory involved in Hitler's equivalent programme. It was Groves's view that the destruction of Vemork was a priority ranking above all others. Under intense pressure from him, the US government overcame its moral, political and humanitarian anxieties and consented to his demands for an air raid. The task was handed to the US 8th Air Force, and the Norwegian government-in-exile and the Norwegian High Command were neither consulted at the planning stage nor even informed that the raid was to take place.

On 16 November, an air fleet of 300 Flying Fortresses and Liberators took off from US bases in East Anglia, heading for Vemork. Some of these planes advanced to two separate targets near Stavanger and Oslo with the aim of diverting German fighters sent up to intercept them. The attacks had been planned to take place at lunchtime, when almost all the workers would have left the plant. As 162 of the bombers flew inland towards Vemork they split into seven formations, and after pinpointing the narrow Rjukan valley they darkened the skies and shook the air as they flew up from the south-west. As they approached the target area, the commander of the Vemork raid realised that they had arrived about twenty minutes too early and that the workers would still be in the plant. Aware of the human and political consequences of an attack at that moment, he ordered the entire fleet to turn back before returning to drop their bombs at the scheduled time.

The decision undoubtedly saved the lives of many innocent Norwegians, but it also removed any element of surprise and allowed the Germans to prepare themselves for the inevitable blitz.

From 12,000 feet, the planes dropped 711 1,000-pound bombs and 201 500-pound bombs in just forty-five minutes.

Armageddon had arrived in the sleepy Norwegian valley. There was pandemonium and devastation on the ground as explosions ripped around the plant and giant billows of smoke and flame shot up from the dark floor of the valley and into the clear bright skies above. The smoke and exhaust fumes of the aircraft caused poor visibility, obscuring the view of the plant for all the planes that followed and resulting in hundreds of bombs missing their targets, some by a matter of miles. Thirteen planes returned to England having refrained from dropping their bombs on account of being unable to see the target. In the chaos, twelve bombers were ordered to divert from the other targets and between them dropped a further 118 500-pound bombs on a nearby target. Two planes, with a total of twenty crew, were lost during the raid, both to engine failure.

Once the details of the damage had been assessed, it became clear that the heavy water high-concentration cells, the priority target, had escaped intact. The roof of the hydro plant in which the stocks were housed was damaged, as were the penstocks behind the plant. A bomb splinter had punctured one high-concentration cell, but the sum total of heavy water destroyed was just 60 kilograms. Out of the 1,000 or so bombs dropped, only 18 hit the Vemork plant. The neighbouring power station received four hits, destroying the roof and two generators.

Six houses next to the plant were completely destroyed and the suspension bridge connecting the plant to the road over the bridge was knocked out. An air-raid shelter full of terrified women and children was also struck. The most unlucky victim was a man skiing up on the mountains several kilometres from the target. He was in the middle of nowhere, one of the loneliest places on the planet, when he was caught by an explosion. In all twenty-two innocent Norwegians were killed. Despite the devastation, the local newspaper, the *Rjukan Dagblad*, was still able to produce its Wednesday edition by the following morning and provided, via SOE's intelligence sources, the first information about the damage caused.

The Norwegian authorities back in London were incandescent with rage. To their credit, they kept their fury confined to the corridors of power, fearful of criticising the Allies and stirring up public anger at the operation. But they left the British and American authorities in no doubt as to their indignation at what had happened in a long, eloquent statement for internal circulation. It began mildly enough: 'The Norwegian Government are fully aware of the necessity of the war being prosecuted with the utmost vigour right up to the moment when the last resistance of the enemy is broken. ...'

The Norwegians went on to point out how they had done their utmost to help the Allies in providing information about the country's industrial plants and other installations and in agreeing to and taking part in the destruction of some of these sites. The implication seemed to be that that help might not be so freely forthcoming in the future, since the Allies had decided that their opinion was surplus to requirements. Also, the statement made clear that the Norwegian authorities had turned their attention to the preservation of their economic industries so that they did not return to a bankrupt nation with its infrastructure ripped out by a combination of Allied attacks and German 'scorch-and-burn' tactics on their withdrawal from the country.

The letter continued: 'The bombing of Norsk Hydro plants at Vemork, the measures taken, seem to be far out of proportion to the objects achieved. ... it took place without the previous knowledge of the Norwegians authorities. No reason has been given to them indicating the necessity of the complete destruction of the works.'

The Norwegians claimed it would have made far more sense to have carried out another raid similar to the one that had been so successful in February, and that they would have been fully prepared to have conducted such an assault with their own men. In what amounted to a diplomatic ear-bashing for the British and Americans, the Norwegians told them it was stupid to think that they had any chance of destroying the 'heavy water' as it was kept underneath the heavily reinforced concrete factory. It should have been realised at the planning stage, they said, that it was 'impossible' to obliterate the stocks through aerial bombardment. Events bore out this assertion. The might of 200 US bombers did not even come close to destroying the main target. The letter went on:

> The bombing of the Norsk Hydro works has made the deepest impression both on the great loyal population in Norway and on the Norwegians fighting with their Allies on the outer battlefronts ... Messages received from Norway testify to the full to the bewilderment and dismay prevailing there. When one knows the enthusiasm with which other offensive actions against targets in Norway have been greeted, these reactions must be considered very seriously ... In making the above observations, the Norwegian Government must express their most profound regret at the events which took place.

Tronstad, too, was upset that he was not even consulted, especially after the enormous contribution he had made to the Allied war efforts in Norway. But his response was colder and more dispassionate, and he calmly pointed out in a letter that the issue was not so much that the Allies had acted in an underhand, morally shabby manner, but that they had been deeply foolish to attack the plant by air if their objective was to retard German efforts to build the bomb. He reminded the Allied authorities that as long ago as July he had told two colonels of the USAAF that they had no chance of destroying the stocks by bombing and that any such action would be a waste of effort and resources and ran the risk, borne out, that dozens of innocent lives would be lost. He had told the Americans that it would be far more sensible to bomb the Skarfoss dam, which would wipe out the plant without killing anyone in the town.

Tronstad, who said he first heard of the raid when he turned on his wireless, tersely pointed out that he had been given every reassurance that plans for a bombing raid would not be tabled without consulting him and his compatriots first. But his key point was that the bombing raid had been entirely counterproductive in that the Germans would now simply transfer all the stock and the apparatus from Vemork, probably to Germany, where it would be far less vulnerable to sabotage.

If the bombing raid had been a tragedy for the people of Rjukan and a blow to Allied–Norwegian relations, it was also a pyrrhic strategic victory for the United States and Britain in their quest to undermine or destroy Germany's progress in building the bomb. They had succeeded in stopping production at Vemork, but what would happen now? Where would the new production plant be installed, and would the Allies' saboteurs or air forces be able to get their bombs on it?

The first inkling that there were German plans afoot to move heavy water and its production facilities out of Norway came from an intercepted letter from a Stockholm bank to the Norwegian legation in the Swedish capital. Four days before Christmas, Swallow telegrammed London to confirm that 'According to information in hand the whole production at Rjukan will stop and the German troops will be replaced by watchmen of the Norwegian S.S. Nothing but the ammonia production can be started again. I will inform you as soon as it is decided what is to be repaired.'

Towards the end of January 1944 Swallow confirmed that the Germans were preparing to dismantle the operation and send all the heavy water to Germany. The news caused great alarm in London and Washington and memos were circulated to the effect that every effort should be made to intercept and destroy the heavy water at any opportunity along its route, first by train and ferry and then ship from Vemork to Hamburg. The correspondence stressed that attempts at its destruction should be made regardless of the dire reprisals that were likely to be visited upon the local population. One memo read: 'The responsible British authorities have decided that in view of the importance of the matter an attack should be tried to be carried out even if serious consequences for the civil Norwegian population may be involved.'

On 7 February Skinnarland wired through another message saying that his contact at the plant had told him the removal was to take place in about a week's time. The information was immediately relayed to Churchill's War Cabinet in London. The message came back that the destruction of the stocks was a 'top priority' – on no account was the heavy water to leave Norway.

The Norwegian government, albeit infuriated that it was not even consulted about the US bombing raid, granted its permission to carry out the attack despite the great risk of reprisals. Within an hour of the news reaching London, Swallow received a reply ordering him to organise an attack.

Tronstad was told of the decision in a solemn letter from SOE on 8 February which read: '... I have to inform you that this proposal has been laid before the highest authorities. The possible repercussions of such an attack on the civilian population have been brought to the notice of the gentlemen in question. I have, however, to inform you that notwithstanding this, the gentlemen in question are of the opinion that such an attempt should be made.'

On 12 February, Haukelid, the only member of Gunnerside to have remained in the area, was tracked down by Skinnarland and summoned from his hiding place 50 kilometres away at a hut called Bamsebu, where he had spent most of the last twelve months. Skinnarland passed on a telegram from London, giving Haukelid the order to destroy the stocks and warning him that the attack must not fail as the Germans would increase still further their vigilance in guarding the heavy water. London also ordered the saboteurs to leave British uniform effects at a suitable place so as to minimise the risk of local reprisals.

With just one week, at the most, before the stocks began their transit from Vemork, Haukelid had very little time to carry out thorough reconnaissance and come up with a comprehensive plan of attack. To make matters worse, the Germans had recently increased their patrols in the mountains and Haukelid's journey from his hideout down to the target area was an especially hazardous one. It was obvious that he would not be able to carry out the attack by himself as he would need at least two others to act as watchmen and fire cover. The problem was that the rest of the Gunnerside and Swallow party had long since left the area, and Haukelid could not risk using Skinnarland as his intelligence and W/T radio network was a vital link with the outside world.

There were six options on the Allies' table: 1) Blow the flasks at Vemork once they had been filled ready for transport. This was considered too difficult as they could be certain that a heavy German guard would be present. 2) Attack the train carrying the stocks from Vemork down to the ferry. This was possible, but there was no guarantee that the heavy water would be destroyed. 3) Blow up the ferry once it had left. Laying the charges would be a highly risky venture, but if successful, the stocks would be lost for ever at the bottom of the lake. 4) Blow up the train on the other side, just north of the town of Notodden. But this had the same flaws as option 2. 5) Launch an attack as the cargo sat waiting at dock to be loaded on to a ship for Germany. Once the cargo was stationary, though, a strong guard was likely to be posted. 6) Sink the ship by air or submarine on its way to Hamburg. This would be a last throw of the die if all other means had failed.

A message was also sent to other special forces and resistance agents in the south of Norway to head to Skien to watch for the arrival of the cargo there. Orders were passed back to resistance men inside the plant to arrange, as far as possible, for the stocks to be on the one ferry to leave the tiny port of Mal on Lake Tinnsjø on Sunday, 20 February. This would help SOE plan a schedule of possible attacks farther down the line.

Skinnarland sent confirmation that all the heavy water stocks were set to be put on the ferry, called *Hydro*, on the day that had been suggested. The option of blowing up the train as it left Vemork was ruled out, leaving Haukelid with just one alternative: he would somehow have to infiltrate the dock area at Mäl, get on board the ferry unnoticed, lay the charges in such a way and place as to ensure that the boat and its cargo would sink quickly, and then make his escape. There could be no risk that the crippled boat might limp into shallow water from where the stocks of heavy water might be saved.

If the logistical aspect of this operation was daunting, the moral conundrum was even more complicated. Innocent lives would certainly be lost. The ferry provided the principal link to the main railway network and was frequently used by local inhabitants. During the war years public transport, like food and other commodities, was severely restricted, and when the ferry did make a journey it was invariably full. It was widely accepted by the generation that lived through the Second World War that painful sacrifices often had to be made for the greater good. But the plan to blow up the *Hydro* stretched that belief to the limit. Rjukan and its satellite hamlets formed a small, tight-knit community. Some of those who would board the ferry on Sunday morning may well have been known to Skinnarland and the Swallow members who had grown up in the area, and it was as well that none of these men was in a position to be called upon to carry out the attack.

Haukelid, who now looked a true wild man of the mountains with his thick beard and weather-beaten face, left his hideaway on 13 February, 1944. Three other men helped him to carry the weapons and explosives needed for the raid. One of these men was Rolf Sørlie, who worked for the resistance, and on their arrival in the Rjukan area he and Haukelid headed into town to see what they could learn about the German plans and their likely strength in numbers during the transit of the stock (Haukelid had shaved, washed and put on clean clothes so as not to arouse suspicion). It did not look promising. The Gestapo had arrived in town in significant numbers to bolster the army and local police contingent, while the local resistance leadership had left the area for one reason or another. The Germans, they learned, had been told to expect an attack at some point during the transport. The managers of the plant had been visited by the Gestapo and warned to be on their guard about a possible raid. The finger was on the trigger.

Sørlie had agreed to help Haukelid in planting the explosives on the ferry, but two more men were needed, they decided. Acting on Skinnarland's recommendations, Haukelid approached Alf Larsen, the chief engineer at the plant, who readily agreed to take part, provided he could join him in escaping to Sweden. Haukelid also brought in a local workman, who had also been recommended by Skinnarland. But on the night of the 14th he failed to return after Haukelid sent him to fetch some equipment from a hut in the hills. Haukelid said he discovered later that the man had run away because he was frightened.

Sørlie was keen to take an active role in the raid, but having not had the proper training he would have been little use if the party became involved in a firefight. Another 'gun' was needed, so a fourth man, Leif Knudsen, yet another engineer at Vemork, was chosen. But in the countdown to the raid, it was realised that his participation in the attack would almost certainly compromise his life and the lives of his family. He would be a prime suspect in any investigation by the Gestapo, so it was decided that he should acquire a false doctor's note saying he was suffering from acute appendicitis and would be taken away to hospital the day before. In his place, Skinnarland recommended Knut Lier-Hansen, another resistance man working for Norsk Hydro, who would join Haukelid and Larsen in the escape to Sweden. Lier-Hansen was a former sergeant in the Norwegian Infantry Regiment who was captured during fighting around Kristiansand after the German invasion on 9 April 1940. He immediately escaped and returned to his home town, Rjukan, where he joined the anti-air-craft battery until the Germans arrived on 4 May. From then on he set about organising resistance, while continuing to work at the Norsk Hydro plant.

Only Sørlie, of the four, would remain in the area.

Haukelid asked Larsen and Gunnar Syverstad, the transport manager at Vemork, who worked for the resistance, to ensure that the cargo was prepared in such a way that it would defi-nitely make the Sunday ferry. Sunday was the best day because generally there was only one trip, and there was therefore no chance of the Germans deciding to wait for a later journey. Moreover, on Sunday, the day of rest, there were likely to be fewer innocent civilians on board. It would also allow Larsen to take part in the operation as he did not work at the plant on Sundays.

Haukelid figured that there were only two courses of action open to him. He could try to seek the cooperation of the engine-room staff in placing the explosives, but it was very unlikely that they would sanction the probable deaths of local people. The only viable strategy was to place a time bomb on board which would sink the ferry before it could make its way to shore. This, however, was fraught with its own obvious risks because the plan would be immediately scuppered if they were discovered by the guards at the dock. But with time rapidly running out, he finally resolved upon this plan on the 17th, just three days before the stock was scheduled to leave.

Another problem was that there were no time-delay devices in the equipment that the British had dropped in their supply runs to the Hardangervidda. So Haukelid went to the workshop of a 'true Norwegian' called John Diseth and built two time delays using alarm clocks. If all went to plan, the alarm-bell hammer would trigger the explosion, but this would be a highly delicate operation as it ran the risk of a sharp movement of the boat setting off the device at any time before the *Hydro* reached deep water or had even been loaded with the cargo. Hauklelid was also lacking electric detonators, but he managed to get hold of some from a local agent called Hjort. For four days, Haukelid and Sørlie prepared themselves for the attack, working by night and sleeping up in the mountains by day.

On 18 February Haukelid made a reconnaissance trip to the ferry to discover where and how best he could lay the charges. In the holds in the engine room he discovered a watertight compartment in the bow of the boat. Here a large enough hole would quickly fill the ship and cause it to tip forward so that the freight carriages carrying the cargo would plunge straight into the water. Haukelid was racked by anxieties about the fate of the innocent passengers, and he pondered an alternative plan of laying a charge to put the engines out of action and stop the boat reaching shore. A second device would then blow a smaller hole, which would make the boat sink slowly and give the passengers a better chance of escaping. At the deepest part of the lake, where the explosion was to take place, the boat would still be no more than a few hundred metres from the shore, and locals would quickly be able to reach the passengers in the water. In the end, however, Haukelid was forced to accept the fact that he was under orders to ensure the destruction of the stocks by the quickest and most effective means. It would have to be Plan A.

On the night of the 18th the Germans began to prepare the transport of the heavy water stocks amid tight security. The thirty-nine drums of heavy water were loaded on to the freight carriages under the glare of giant night lamps while a heavy guard surrounded the operation. It was obvious that the saboteurs would have had no chance of launching a successful attack here and had been right to choose the ferry option.

On Saturday, the entire consignment was transported to Rjukan railway station ready to be taken down to Mael ferry port the following morning. At 0100 hours Haukelid, Sørlie, Larsen, Lier-Hansen and a driver they knew they could trust set out from Rjukan in a car they had hired for the short but fraught journey down the only road to Mal. One of the remarkable features of this action was that Haukelid had never met any of his colleagues, other than Sørlie, until just two days earlier. SOE agents normally acted only under the tightest rules of security, but it is a measure of Haukelid's determination and the importance of the operation that he was prepared to risk betrayal and capture in order to carry out his mission.

On arrival, they parked the car out of sight off the road and set off by foot to the ferry, leaving Larsen sitting in the car with instructions to go after two hours if the others had not returned.

They could see the freight carriages sitting on the dockside, lit up by bright floodlights, as they strolled towards the boat, acting as if they were members of its crew. A stoker working in the engine room saw the party enter but he said nothing and continued his work. The rest of the crew was involved in a raucous poker game at the other end of the boat.

Incredibly, there appeared to be no German on the boat or guarding entry to it, but when they went down to the passenger cabin they were immediately confronted by a Norwegian a little worse for drink. It was a heart-stopping moment for the raiders. Was this man a quisling or a patriot? They gambled and told him they were Jøssings ('good Norwegians') on the run and needed somewhere to hide their belongings until the coast was clear. It was an ingenious piece of improvisation by Haukelid as it gave him an excuse for descending into the bowels of the ship. 'Thank God he was a true Norwegian too,' he recorded.

No matter how patriotic the man was, however, there was little chance he would be party to the ship's destruction with the likely loss of his crewmates even if he understood the vital importance of the operation. Lier-Hansen stayed with the man called John Berg – he knew him from the local sports club and kept him chatting as Haukelid and Sørlie descended to the third-class deck, from where they wriggled through a hole in the floor into the bowels of the ship with their rucksacks of explosives and home-made timers.

It was a struggle as they crawled through one foot of water along the keel towards the bow. There was just half a metre of clearance between the water and the ceiling, which made the laying of the explosives that much more difficult and perilous.

Haukelid had already prepared a 'sausage' containing 8.4 kilograms of explosive, large enough to blow a hole that would sink the boat in about four or five minutes. With the explosive strapped to the wall of the boat, Haukelid set the alarm for 1045 hours, but with just two millimetres' clearance between the bell hammer and the detonator this was a heart-thumpingly nervous moment for the pair. (Haukelid later admitted it was a little 'ticklish'.) Upstairs, Lier-Hansen was growing anxious about his colleagues' progress, while in the car Larsen nervously fingered his watch, beginning to fear that the party had been discovered by the Germans. If they were captured, Larsen knew they would probably be interrogated under torture and then executed.

As Larsen prepared to start for home, to his relief the three men appeared and jumped into the car. It was exactly 0400 hours, the time he had been told to leave if they had not appeared. Haukelid and Larsen were to drive to Jondalen from where they would catch the train to Oslo before making contact with an escape party to guide them to the Swedish frontier. In the original plan, Lier-Hansen was to go with them but on the night he changed his mind, saying he would risk returning to Rjukan to check that the containers had not been removed from the ferry and, if they had, to remove the charges and prevent the needless deaths of innocent civilians. They had escaped from the immediate danger area, but there was still plenty to worry about. Had the Germans used the freight train as a dummy consignment and sent the heavy water stocks by car? Would they decide to delay the journey until the following day, knowing that the Norwegian resistance would have been aware of the stocks having been taken to Mal? Would Haukelid's home-made devices work? Would they explode too soon and allow the containers to be recovered from shallow water?

These were their thoughts as the train rattled towards Oslo the following morning. At 10.45 Haukelid looked at his watch and wondered. If everything had gone to plan, how many innocent people had just died? But how many more tens of thousands might he just have saved?

The following morning Skinnarland hurried out from his hideaway to find a copy of the Quisling newspaper *Fritt Folk*, which ran a banner headline announcing the sinking of the ferry and reported that all the rail carriages had slid into the freezing water at the deepest point of the lake, just as Haukelid had planned, and that several people had died, just as he had feared. Skinnarland sent the following telegram to London: 'The Ferry was sunk on Sunday. Unfortunately some people drowned. Our people are OK. Bonzo [code name for Haukelid] has gone to Sweden. Our contact engineer Larsen has also left for Sweden where I hope he will be given a good reception.'

Another telegram from SOE in Stockholm confirmed the news, stating that the ferry had gone down in three minutes 300 metres into the lake (at its deepest point) with the loss of eighteen lives, fourteen Norwegian and four German. Among the dead were a couple from Notodden and their three-year-old daughter. Most of those who died had been below deck in the cheaper seats when the explosion ripped through the boat.

Nineteen people were rescued by farmers and fishermen, who rowed to the scene on hearing the explosion and seeing the 493-ton vessel slip beneath the surface of the icy water. One of the rescuers was an eighty-year-old called Gudleik Persgaard, who made two trips to the site and saved several lives. The drunk crew member who the party had encountered was saved by the boat's stoker who carried him ashore a few hours before it departed.

Erling Sørensen, the captain of the *Hydro*, survived the attack and later recalled the moment the charges exploded: 'At around 10:30 I was on the bridge and I heard an explosion. It definitely sounded like a bomb. The ship went over on to the port side and after a few minutes it was lying flat on its side. I walked along the ship's side as it if was a floor and after taking my coat off – I forgot to take my boots off – I jumped into the water and swam about fifteen feet away. I turned around and watched her go down. The stern was very high and the propeller was still going around when she went down.'

Later four barrels bobbed to the surface and were recovered by the Germans. This baffled everyone back at SOE headquarters – how could heavy water float? But the mystery was resolved when intelligence from the engineers at the plant explained that these barrels were less than half full because there was only a small amount of some concentrations. Moreover, the heavy water in the barrels, totalling just 87 kilograms, was of such low concentration that it was as good as useless to the Germans.

The success of Haukelid's daring coup was greeted with joy in London and Washington. Once and for all, Germany's only significant source of material for an atomic bomb had been destroyed – or at least put beyond its reach. Over 3,600 gallons of the laboriously produced fluid were now sitting on the bed of Lake Tinnsjø, 400 metres below the surface. It was a crippling blow for Hitler and his Nazi war machine, as there was no longer any realistic chance that they would beat the Americans and the British in the race to build the bomb. The fighting in western

Europe would continue for another fifteen months, but the tide
of success had already turned to the Allies' advantage and they,
not the Germans, would soon have possession of a weapon the
threat or use of which would bring about victory and a swift end
to the bloodiest conflict in history.

10

What Rewards for These Heroic Men?

The Germans, predictably, were furious that their heavy security measures had been breached and the stock of heavy water lost for ever. The locals anxiously awaited the backlash, their fears mounting as more and more Gestapo and Norwegian Hirdmen swept into town. There were a number of arrests, but for the first two weeks the Germans reserved judgement, not wanting to admit publicly or to the authorities in Berlin that the ferry had been sunk by sabotage. They, too, feared reprisals, which most probably would take the form of a transfer to the hell of the Eastern Front.

Syverstad, the laboratory assistant and resistance fighter who had assisted Haukelid at the start of the ferry operation, escaped across the border to Sweden with the Gestapo hot on his trail. He was sought in the mountains and had watched his hut being bombed from the air as he fled. During his debriefing with SOE in Stockholm he said the Germans were 'altogether in a nasty temper' and that a Gestapo officer called Munkenthaler, who was permanently based in the town, had told residents that 'Rjukan would be made to weep this time'. Munkenthaler had also given a stark warning to a man called Fredriksen, one of Syverstad's colleagues at the plant, saying that, if he tried to escape, 'I will blow up your villa with your wife in it.'

In the end, all those arrested and interrogated were released and the Germans reported that the sinking of the ferry was probably caused by an accidental explosion in the engine room, thus absolving themselves of any blame in its loss. They did weep in Rjukan after all, but they were tears of relief and joy.

Larsen told SOE during his debriefing in London that Haukelid 'showed him the care of a mother to her child' during their escape to Sweden. While they were in Stockholm waiting to be flown to England, a telegram was received by the SOE agent there, asking him to inform Haukelid that the British had awarded him the Distinguished Service Order (DSO) for his gallantry.

There were, however, growing concerns for Lier-Hansen, who had bravely decided to return to the area to remove the explosive charges if this had become necessary. Within days of the ferry sinking, intelligence emerged that the Gestapo had targeted him as a suspect and plans were hastily made to evacuate him to Sweden.

Once the furore over the ferry sinking had subsided, Haukelid went back to the Telemark region and linked up with Skinnarland and Sørlie to continue the fight for their country's liberation. Helberg, Poulsson, Haugland and Kjelstrup were later dropped back on to the Hardangervidda to prepare for the final push to oust the invaders, while Rønneberg and the other members of the original attack at Vemork took part in other SOE operations in Norway until the war was over.

Nine months before liberation day in Norway, Skinnarland had sent a message to London, informing them that all the apparatus used for the production of heavy water had been packed up under the noses of the Norwegians and driven away from the plant, bound, they were told, for somewhere in Germany or Austria. Clearly, Hitler's atomic programme had not been terminated, but the wider intelligence indicated that they were so off the pace established by the American scientists that the threat was no longer considered significant.

On 16 July 1945 the world's first A-bomb was exploded in the New Mexico desert. It was four times more powerful than scientists had expected, and the sand where it landed was blasted into green glass by the intensity of the explosion. On 6 August, the US bomber *Enola Gay*, captained by Mark Tibbets, dropped a uranium bomb over the Japanese city of Hiroshima. Three days later, a plutonium bomb with the power of 20,000 tons of TNT was dropped over Nagasaki. Over 140,000 were killed in the two blasts and millions were injured or made homeless. The Second World War was over, but the apocalypse had arrived.

Today, we talk of Hiroshima and Nagasaki as the benchmark of horror, but it might well have been London, Birmingham or Bristol. We know now that by the end of the war Hitler's atomic bomb programme, which was so advanced at the start of hostilities, had fallen far behind the United States' Manhattan Project. The questions 'how far' and 'why' remain in dispute among historians. Some have claimed that the programme was deliberately stalled by good men within the German scientific community working on the project, but this theory has been largely discredited. The saturation bombing of Germany's industrial interests by Allied bombers certainly hampered progress, while the flight of the country's Jewish physicists at the start of the war left a vacuum of knowledge that was never filled. Bad science and technical incompetence were also factors, but the Germans' failure to get their hands on Vemork's heavy water was undoubtedly a major blow to the programme.

The textbook sabotage raid by the Gunnerside and Swallow parties not only destroyed stocks of the vital material, its timing was also crucial. It was planned and carried out at roughly the same time that the war was slowly turning against Hitler. Germany began to reel under the intensive carpet bombing of its major cities and industrial installations, while its military fronts began to crack and crumble under the pressure of reinvigorated Allied offensives. The destruction of the heavy water stocks, first at Vemork and then on Lake Tinnsjø, compounded the general and growing sense of hopelessness among German scientists. While their rivals in the United States were spurred on by the momentum generated by success on the battlefield and the real hope of ultimate victory, the German physicists became aware that they were struggling for a doomed cause.

The men of Swallow and Gunnerside were, of course, entirely unaware of this terrible race going on behind the scenes, and in a way this makes the courage of their actions that much more remarkable. Colonel Jack Wilson, the head of SOE's Norwegian section, wrote after the war: 'It was nearly 18 months before even many of those who had taken part in the various actions realised to the full the great value of the work they had done. To those in the know, and there were very, very few, it was a most anxious time.'

There is no doubt that the Gunnerside party were in very great danger in that first week after their arrival, and there is no doubt that Grouse were in great difficulties during those terrible few weeks without basic rations in the teeth of one of the Hardangervidda's most severe winters. But the survivors of both parties have always played down these experiences, just as they play down virtually every single one of their achievements in the story.

In all the dozens of interviews they have given on the subject, not once do you read or hear any of them talking up their achievement. On the contrary, they try to give the impression that what they achieved was perfectly unremarkable. To read their accounts of what happened or listen to them talk about it today is to be given a lesson in modesty and understatement. Their humility, as a group and as individuals, astonishes. The eleven men involved in the Vemork raid are heroes in Norway, but you get sharply rebuked if you dare suggest that to them. (Their stock reply is that it was the people of Norway living under occupation, or the men who died in the Freshman disaster, who are the real heroes.) Whether that is the way of the Norwegian and/or the soldier, or whether their modesty is something peculiar to them, is difficult to say.

These were strong, tough men who pushed themselves to the limits of human endurance and courage for the liberation of their country. During the hardest times, the saboteurs' focus was the destruction of the heavy water plant. That was their mission and they wanted to carry it out as professionals. But they had another, even more important objective: they wanted their country back. It is difficult for us to imagine today what it must have been like living under a ruthless occupying enemy, but the loss of freedom, the disruption of families, the deprivation of life's basic requirements, let alone its luxuries, living in a constant state of terror and amid the deaths of loved ones, provided an overwhelmingly powerful motivation for these young Norwegians, just as it did for other people across Europe.

Today we are no longer forced to push ourselves; life in the West is very comfortable for the vast majority of its people. The great survival stories may appear to have little relevance to those of us living in a cosy Western home today, but they can still be read as a metaphor, an inspiration, for our own struggle in life, whatever that may be. Perhaps we should let this story speak for itself – a true story of incredible courage, fortitude, daring, resourcefulness, military skill, brotherhood, self-sacrifice, patriotism and outdoormanship – but if there is any lesson to be drawn from the triumphs of its main characters, it is that only by pushing himself to the very limits of his endurance for the sake of others can a man be said to have truly lived.

Hidden inside a tatty cardboard folder among thousands of other faded documents in the vaults of the Public Record Office in Kew is a small scrap of paper with a simple question typed across the middle. 'What rewards are to be given to these heroic men?' it asks. The heading on the paper gives the address as 10 Downing Street, Whitehall, and it is dated 14.4.43. It is signed W.S.C. in the only ink on the page. Churchill, who had taken an active interest in the Telemark venture over the previous twelve months, had just read the first official report into the sabotage raid at Vemork. He must have felt like ordering himself a whisky and heavy water to celebrate – with heavy water ice cubes, of course.

Shortly afterwards, King George VI approved the following awards:

OBE
Captain and Professor Leif Tronstad

DSO (Distinguished Service Order)
Second Lieutenant Jens Anton Poulsson
Second Lieutenant Joachim Holmboe Rønneberg

MC (Military Cross)
Second Lieutenant Knut Magne Haugland
Second Lieutenant Kasper Idland
Second Lieutenant Knut Anders Haukelid

MM (Military Medal)
Sergeant Claus Urbye Helberg
Sergeant Arne Kjelstrup
Sergeant Fredrik Thorbjørn Kayser
Sergeant Hans Storhaug
Sergeant Birger Edvan Martin Strømsheim

Skinnarland was later awarded the Distinguished Conduct Medal while Dr Brun was awarded the MBE. Haukelid, as noted earlier, was also awarded the DSO after blowing up the *Hydro* ferry. Alf Larsen was awarded the OBE, Gunnar Syverstad received the British Empire Medal, while Major-General Gubbins was knighted and Colonel Wilson was given an OBE. (Gubbins went on to receive a chestful of medals from all the countries SOE helped liberate.) All the Norwegians between them received a countless number of other decorations and awards from Norway and several other countries, and they remain heroes in their country to this day.

In recommending awards, Major-General Gubbins, the head of SOE, wrote: 'Where the essence of an operation is teamwork the singling out of individuals for recognition is both invidious and hateful.'

Of Rønneberg he wrote: '... showed a spirit of persistence and cool, calm courage which is beyond all praise. He was fully alive to all the difficulties and dangers of his position and demonstrated the virtues of steadiness and inspiration in a high degree.' Of the retreat to Sweden he said: 'His display of tactics, fieldcraft and snowcraft was most marked.'

Of Poulsson, Gubbins said: 'As leader [of Grouse/Swallow] he showed a spirit of persistence that is beyond all praise.' Of Haugland, he wrote: 'He has at least an equal share in the credit for the excellent service rendered by the advance party. Despite the most trying conditions, his transmission was maintained at a first-class standard. ... His coolness and sense of humour have been most remarkable during the whole time that he has been exposed to danger from the elements and from the enemy.'

All eleven men involved in the Grouse/Swallow and Gunnerside operations survived the war. Rønneberg, Poulsson, Strømsheim, Haugland and Kayser are still alive.

JOACHIM RØNNEBERG

In the summer of 1943 Rønneberg began a long operation in the north of Norway where he remained until March 1945, when severe stomach trouble forced him to return to Britain. He chose Strømsheim and another man he knew from his childhood to join him on the mission to prepare themselves for the possible arrival of Allied troops and to carry out sabotage acts on vital German installations. Together they lived up in the mountains in terrible conditions similar to those experienced by the Grouse party on the Hardangervidda. 'To be honest, that year and a half, living in an unheated hut or out in the open with little food and very low temperatures, was far more demanding than the Vemork trip,' Rønneberg recalled. 'I am very glad to have made so many strong friendships during these operations in the war. They became stronger than they were before and that tells you something about the characters who were involved.' After the war Rønneberg was involved in broadcasting and became known as the 'Voice of Norway'. He later became a television and radio producer while giving military lectures to, among others, the Norwegian army and the British SAS.

JENS ANTON POULSSON

Poulsson returned to Norway in 1944, recruiting and training hundreds of Norwegians for the Home Forces. He remained in the army and rose to the rank of colonel, an expert in mountain warfare and arctic survival. Living in Kongsberg, halfway between Rjukan and Oslo, and still a keen outdoorsman despite his advancing years, he has continued to spend a lot of time up on the Hardangervidda.

CLAUS HELBERG

Helberg too returned to Telemark and became a radio operator as well as an instructor for the Home Forces. After the war he returned to his work with the Norwegian Mountaineering Association and became a senior figure in the country's tourist industry. A friend to the royal families of Norway, Sweden and Denmark, Helberg was a living legend in Norway. He died at the age of eighty-four in March 2003, a few days after the sixtieth anniversary celebrations of the Vemork raid. He never lost his love for the mountain life and even led a party of skiers along the 'saboteurs' route' in the week before he passed away. His death was mourned throughout Norway, and his funeral was attended by royalty and the country's leading politicians.

KNUT HAUGLAND

Haugland saw out the war in Norway, reinforcing his reputation as one of the Allies' best W/T operators of the entire conflict. He also joined a group of resistance fighters called the 'Oslo Gang', who were regarded by many as the best sabotage team in occupied Europe. Haugland had a long career in the Norwegian Army after the war and was chosen for his wireless skills to take part in the famous Kon-Tiki expedition led by Thor Heyerdahl in 1947. Six of them sailed 3,800 miles on a 13-metre balsa-wood raft from South America to Polynesia to prove Heyerdahl's theory about the migration of early man. He also helped establish and manage the Norwegian Resistance Museum and the Kon-Tiki museum in Oslo.

KNUT HAUKELID

After crossing back over the Swedish frontier following the ferry sinking, Haukelid remained in Norway for the rest of the war, working with the resistance and the Home Forces. He joined the Norwegian Army after the war and rose to the rank of major in the Telemark Infantry Regiment. He was later appointed lieutenant colonel and head of the Home Guard of Greater Oslo. He died in 1994.

EINAR SKINNARLAND

Skinnarland stayed in Norway for the duration of the war after his SOE training in March 1942. On liberation day, he emerged from his hideaway as one of the leaders of the Home Forces in the northern Telemark region. He emigrated to the United States shortly after the war and worked as an engineer on a number of major construction projects around the world. His family continue to run the Skinnarbu hotel close to the Møsvatn dam where he lived as a child and young man. After suffering a stroke a few months earlier, he died in Toronto, Canada, of a brain haemmo-rhage in December 2002. A desperately modest man to the end, he never displayed any of his medals, instead keeping them locked in a safe. One souvenir he did keep with him, however, was the case for the poison pill he was given by SOE before returning to Telemark.

LEIF TRONSTAD

The one central figure of the heavy water story not to see out the war was Professor Leif Tronstad, who did as much as anyone to thwart Hitler's atomic bomb programme. After returning to the region as commander of another SOE operation, he and Syverstad were brutally murdered by a lunatic when he went to interrogate a local magistrate with links to the Norwegian Nazi Party.

APPENDIX

The Norwegian Resistance

By the time the *Hydro* ferry had slid beneath the surface of Lake Tinnsjø, the resistance in Norway had developed into a highly efficient and formidable movement. Each week hundreds of new recruits abandoned their lives under occupation and headed into the mountains to join the training camps hidden up there. The Norwegians were now being supplied with a considerable amount of equipment and weaponry by the RAF, while SOE soldiers and Milorg resistance fighters carried out the training. But to a great extent, the teeth of the Home Forces (*Hjemmefront*) had been drawn by the Allies, who went to great lengths to restrain them from rising up too soon and provoking a savage clampdown by the Germans.

The resistance movement in Norway, which manifested itself in a variety of different forms, was forced to organise itself out of thin air, but after an understandably slow start it quickly began to evolve into a meaningful and effective organisation. After a time, it was to the thousands of men and women who risked their lives to join its ranks that the good Norwegian people looked for inspiration. The movement remains a source of great pride in a country that still feels pangs of guilt and discomfort about the traitor Vidkun Quisling and the small percentage of the population who put their names to the Nazi cause.

Within the space of twenty-four hours following the German blitzkrieg in 1940, the Norwegian government, soon to be exiled in London, lost its moral as well as its real authority. The shock of the invasion, the speed of the occupation and the lack of leadership tainted the country's legitimate administrators. Overnight, they had lost the trust and respect of their people, and it would have been difficult for them to persuade their people from exile that they still retained any right to govern or influence them in the struggle for liberation. In the absence of a true government, people inevitably turned elsewhere for support and hope. It came in the forms of the resistance movement, their British and American allies, the Russian fighting on the Eastern Front, the Norwegian soldiers being trained in the UK, from broadcasts by the BBC and King Haakon VII, and from their own belief that the German forces would ultimately be crushed.

In the summer of 1940 Norway was a defeated, traumatised and confused nation, with neither the leadership nor the means to resist and help drive out the invaders. But what the people did still possess as they surveyed the wreckage of their lives after the invasion was their will to fight. It would take a monumental effort on the part of the people – and their Allies – but slowly a network of resistance would be established and expanded so that by the following year the fight for liberation could begin in earnest. This was to be a secret war, and a war of attrition, waged under the occupation of a brutal regime. Those who fought it would do so at constant risk to their own lives and those of their families and their comrades.

Germany had hoped that King Haakon and his government

would be forced to accept some kind of compromise administration in which they could still have some influence so long as
they cooperated. But King Haakon's response, broadcast by the
BBC's Norwegian service, rebuffed German overtures to 'come
quietly' and enjoy the fruits of the Aryan revolution. Norway's
position was made clear from the outset: there would be no
formal collaboration as there was in Vichy France. The country
would fight for its freedom and sovereign independence, even
though this would mean years of hardship, misery and atrocities.

The Germans were forced to turn to Vidkun Quisling in a bid
to try to bestow some legitimacy on the new administration.
Quisling was loathed by the vast majority of Norwegians, but
he had a small following of diehard loyalists and Aryan fanat-
ics, prepared to surrender the country's sovereignty and betray
their compatriots for the Nazi cause. In late September 1940,
the Reichskommissar Josef Terboven announced the establishment of a new government involving Quisling, but effectively
controlled by Berlin. Quisling's party was called Nasjonal
Samling (National Unification), went by the initials NS and had
about 20,000 members out of a population of three million. Its
legitimisation by the Germans formally drew the line that
would divide Norway over the coming years. On the one side
were the collaborators and the appeasers, on the other the 'true
Norwegians', those prepared to fight for their country's freedom or at least offer passive resistance in the form of non-
cooperation.

The Gestapo, meanwhile, employed their usual methods of
interrogation on political prisoners and captured resistance fighters, using Chinese water torture, leg screws, whips and cudgels on
those unfortunate enough to fall into their grasp.

The German policy in Norway, as elsewhere across occupied Europe, was to try to create acquiescence in the population by a mixture of persuasion and propaganda backed up by a threat of dire consequences for those who offered defiance. They understood that resistance and non-cooperation would tie up troops and slow the economic activity of the country. Four days after the invasion, General von Falkenhorst was presented with an opportunity to lay down the new law for the Norwegians. Two Norwegians blew up a strategically important bridge linking Oslo to the Fornebu airport, and von Falkenhorst immediately ordered hundreds of posters to be pinned up around the city, threatening heavy reprisals on the community and summary execution of the perpetrators of similar acts of defiance in the future. The following day, a group of influential Norwegians published a plea in the newspapers urging all Norwegians not to provoke the Germans into taking repressive action. It amounted to a call for the people to lay down their arms and accept the new regime. In the autumn of 1940 the first resistance group was formed in Oslo, but it did not last long – it was exposed, and those who managed to escape arrest were forced to flee.

The majority of Norwegians remained largely passive throughout the war, but pockets of defiant patriotic young men would grow as the months wore on, while many thousands of others, notably in the Church and the teachers' union, were doggedly uncooperative. Many would simply express their resistance through small acts such as refusing to sit next to Germans on trains or trams, shunning public meetings, throwing the odd stone at a passing vehicle or hissing at gatherings of German troops. These seem ineffectual compared with the active resistance that would be offered by those who took up arms, but they played a part in undermining German morale and legitimacy. Early in the occupation a doctor called Johan Scharffenberg issued a famous call to resistance that was distributed among the people via the underground press network. 'This spiritual tutelage from people not superior in character or in intelligence is like slow strangulation. If this is going to be our condition in Norway, then I must seek comfort in the saying: "*vivere non est necesse*" – to live is no necessity.'

Many good Norwegians, working in institutions such as the police or local government, faced a dreadful moral dilemma: did they publicly register their disapproval by resigning their posts or did they stay and try to have an influence on life from within? Some level of cooperation was needed in order to keep the economy going, not least to ensure there was food on the table and other basic provisions and services for the people. There were Norwegian Nazis on most official committees of all institutions across the country, but they were always in a minority and were spread so disparately and thinly that as a group of people they lacked coordination and focus and thus real power.

The country's leading judges resigned as one after refusing to bow to Terboven's diktats, but it was the combined forces of the Church and the schools which landed the biggest blow against German plans to win over the Norwegians. Early in 1941, the Lutheran State Church, the main religious body in Norway, issued a powerful statement, expressing its contempt for the new administration and rallying the beleaguered population.

When state authorities permit violence and injustice and exert pressure on human souls, then the Church becomes the guardians of consciences. One human soul means more than the whole world. The bishops of the Church have therefore laid on the Ministry's table some facts and official proclamations of recent times concerning the nation's public affairs which the Church finds contrary to the law of God ... Consciences are troubled in our parishes now, and we feel it our duty to give to the men of the State a clear expression of the voice of the Church.

In 1942, 645 of the country's 699 clergymen resigned their office in protest at state interference, rendering the State Church a virtually empty institution without any congregations.

Nor were the teachers prepared to play ball with the Nazis. At first they refused to sign a document pledging loyalty to the new regime, and later 12,000 of the 14,000-strong profession called for open protest against a scheme to institute a Norwegian version of Hitler's youth programme. Their defiance resulted in 1,300 of them being arrested at random and sent to concentration camps.

As the months went by it became increasingly difficult for ordinary Norwegians to avoid stating their true allegiances, and more and more came out into the open to offer civil resistance to the new regime. Among them were the nation's sportsmen, who as early as 1940 went on strike and refused to take part in any form of meaningful competition while they remained under occupation. In early 1941, twenty-two civil service organisations issued a letter of protest to Terboven. Many professionals from all walks of life, including engineers, dentists, lawyers and accountants, resigned their jobs and began to work underground, evolving over time into a kind of parallel, twilight society beneath the official infrastructure. Those who chose to support the Nazi regime, by taking the higher wages on offer to help construct and maintain the Nazi infrastructure, building barracks, airfields, defences and so on, earned the eternal opprobrium of their compatriots. Many thousands would be put on trial after the war to answer charges of collaboration and profiteering.

The great challenge for the Norwegians was in trying to coordinate a resistance movement under such a severely repressive regime, in which freedom had been extinguished, movement and speech restricted, and in which internment, torture or even death awaited those who dared challenge the new authority.

Their king and government were in exile and their army had been scattered to the winds. Offering civil resistance was one thing, but fighting back was a challenge of an altogether greater order of magnitude. Back in Britain, SOE was desperately trying to recruit, train and deploy as many agents as possible to carry out Churchill's plan to 'set Europe ablaze'. But in Norway, pockets of resistance could grow into something more significant only once it had been established that the greater proportion of the country would offer support rather than betrayal. The civil resistance of those first few months and the subsequent 'defection' of so many professionals into the underground were all the encouragement they needed.

There was, however, the problem of coordinating the internal movement with the activities of SOE and SIS. Milorg, the name assumed by the Norwegian resistance, were at first suspicious of SOE, while there were many back in London, not least the government-in-exile, who feared that the resistance movement could fall under the control of communists who would use the war to further their political ambitions. There was considerable tension among resistance groups across Europe, as they were often and to varying degrees riven by their own internal political conflicts and hierarchy jealousies. In France, for example, it was Gaullists versus communists, while in Greece it was monarchists versus communists. Norway had its own fears about communists, but the scale of in-fighting within Milorg was nothing like that of other groups.

Through correspondence, smuggled in and out of the country, the various parties reached an understanding, which put Milorg under the control of the Norwegian High Command, but gave them a largely free hand to continue their operations as they saw fit. It was a triumph for Norwegian common sense, decency and loyalty to the Crown that this loose arrangement was never critically strained throughout the duration of the war, despite the fog of misunderstandings, suspicions and lack of easy communication between the different groups involved.

In September 1941, a snap strike by workers in Oslo, called in protest against the ending of milk rationing, prompted a brutal crackdown by the authorities. Hundreds were arrested, tortured and imprisoned, and some were executed.

Around this time the Germans also ordered that all wireless sets should be handed in, so that the Norwegians could no longer listen to the morale-boosting BBC broadcasts, carrying messages of hope and defiance from King Haakon. The possession of a radio set became punishable by internment under the new directive, but many Norwegians refused to hand in their sets and would listen to them whenever possible, maintaining their only contact with the free world. BBC Radio made a major contribution to the war effort in Norway as well as in countless other countries around the globe. In addition to broadcasting messages from the King and members of his government-in-exile, the BBC also provided practical information to Norwegians about how to survive under occupation and how to offer resistance without endangering themselves.

Many coded messages were also sent to resistance fighters and SOE operatives in apparently harmless BBC broadcasts. The following example, for instance, carried instructions for Skinnarland, although we have no idea what it meant to him. It read:

> A good illustration of the deterioration of German morale amongst the military may be taken from the following story. A German officer recently returned from leave in Germany. When he came back to the Hotel Ernst at Kristiansand, where he had lived for many months before his leave, it was noticed that he tore down a large photograph of Hitler which he had hung up in his room before leaving. The photograph was thrown away on the rubbish dump the following morning.

The clampdown on the use of radio also led to a flourishing of the underground press in Norway, with several new publications, with names such as *The Whispering Times*, secretly produced and distributed throughout the country. Such was the confidence of the patriots that there developed what was known as the 'Ice Front', by which families sympathetic to the Nazi cause were isolated socially.

At first, Norway was a mere outpost of the Nazi empire, strategically important for its naval operations but needing relatively few troops to keep control of the small population. But in 1942 Hitler became convinced that it was here that the Allies would launch an invading force at the start of the campaign to liberate Europe. It was true that Churchill favoured the plan, known as 'Operation Jupiter', to invade Norway, but in the end the Allies felt that first North Africa, then France were the main fronts on which to fight. Between January and June, 150,000 German troops were sent to reinforce 'Festung Norwegen' (Fortress Norway), taking the total to 250,000. (By the end of the war, their number would rise to over 400,000.)

By the end of 1942 SIS, Britain's Secret Intelligence Service, and SOE were firmly established in Norway. SIS, which received its first message from an operative inside Norway as early as 10 June 1940, had sixteen intelligence stations operating in the country, most of them along the long southern and western lengths of its 2,000-mile-long coastline, alerting London to the movements of enemy shipping. SOE carried out twenty-two sabotage actions that year and established thirteen radio operators, sending back their own intelligence. Towards the end of the war the Soviets, whose land bordered Norway up in the Arctic, followed SOE's example and began training saboteurs and W/T operators before dropping them back into the Finnmark region in the very north of the country.

SOE's operations in Norway were highly varied. Anything of vital importance to German interests was attacked, including Norway's substantial pyrite mines and transports of vital cargos by ship and train. In the last year of the war SOE spearheaded a major campaign against German oil and petrol stocks, robbing its U-boat campaign and other military activities of about three million gallons of fuel.

At the outbreak of hostilities dozens of Norwegian fishing boats escaped to Scotland, where the crews offered their services to the Allied war effort. This was a godsend for SOE, which had constant problems persuading the RAF to lend them the use of their aircraft and crews for operations. Like all equipment and goods, aircraft were in severely short supply in the early years of the war, and the vast majority were concentrated on operations in the main theatre of war farther south.

The crews of the 'Shetland Bus' therefore provided a vital passage between Norway and the free world, taking a stream of recruits one way and a column of SOE-trained operatives the other. The boats were perfect because they could mingle with the real Norwegian fishing fleet. The only drawback was that, like those of the RAF, their activities were severely hampered by the seasons. The long daylight hours of summer meant that most operations had to be stopped between March and September, but for two years the Shetland Bus made an immense contribution to the Norwegian and Allied war effort. In 1941–42 six boats made forty-one trips, landing forty-seven agents and 130 tons of stores. Three boats and fourteen men were lost. In 1942–43 they made thirty-seven trips, landing 36 tons and twenty-two agents. Four boats and twenty-five men were lost. Each one of the agents who landed successfully was then able to recruit and train a dozen more volunteers, who in turn were able to do the same, thus giving the resistance movement a powerful momentum that would eventually help to drive the Nazis from their land. By whatever route or means of transport, 3,300 Norwegians reached the UK in 1940 and 1941. A further 300 died in shipwrecks or were captured.

In a War Cabinet memorandum on SOE operations in Scandinavia, circulated in May 1945, it was stated: 'It would be impossible to praise too highly the courage and devotion of these Norwegians in carrying SOE agents to and from Norway through the many dangers at sea, off shore and on land.' Like the British and Norwegian merchant sailors, who lost men in their thousands trying to bring vital supplies to the Allies, the men of the Shetland Bus were among the great unsung heroes of the conflict.

The Germans eventually all but outlawed fishing in an effort to neutralise contact with Britain, thus making any fishing vessel a target for attack. The small boats were unable to defend themselves, particularly from the air. From the summer of 1943, the Americans gave SOE three submarine-chasers, which were fast and silent, perfect vessels for their operations. In the six months from November 1943 they made thirty-four trips to Norway, landing forty agents and 22 tons of stores.

In an attempt to prevent more Norwegians fleeing into the mountains and more remote regions where they could join the resistance, the Germans also put up posters ordering the population to hand in all outdoor gear, including gumboots, tents, rucksacks, wind-proof clothing and blankets. The penalty for failure to comply was three years in prison.

The RAF also played a major part in SOE's operations and the support of the Norwegian resistance movement. In November 1944 alone, for example, services by air – and some by sea – supplied to Norway 53 tons of general stores, 1,628 rifles, 322 carbines, eight bazookas, 120 Bren guns, 860 Sten guns and 1,014 grenades. In the early years of the war, the Norwegian resistance suffered from a lack of basic equipment and weapons, but in the final year they had enough following the hundreds of drops carried out by the RAF. 'We never had an opportunity of thanking in person those fellows who came over on moonlit nights,' Haukelid said after the war. 'They gave us what we needed to support life. Those great heavy planes were the link between us and the free world.'

Milorg had suffered a near-mortal blow in the autumn of 1941 after they had been exposed by an infiltrator and subjected to a savage crackdown by the Gestapo. But those who escaped the purge managed to regroup, and together with the various agents from 'outside' they began to cause serious trouble for the German war machine, tying up troops, disrupting transport links and destroying vital military supplies and equipment.

Infiltration was a constant fear for Milorg, and in February 1942 they suffered one of the heaviest setbacks of the war when the notorious informer Henry Oliver Rinnan exposed an entire resistance group on the west coast. The German reaction was brutal: eighteen men were executed and the town of Televåg with its 300 houses was destroyed. All fishing vessels were sunk, the cattle killed or confiscated, and the entire male population was transported to concentration camps in Germany while the rest of the inhabitants were interned in camps in Norway. An ancient community was effectively annihilated in a matter of days.

From 1943 onwards, when the tide of the war had begun to turn against the Axis powers, the authorities in London began to prepare plans for a full-scale invasion of Norway. The liberation of the country, when it came, would be a process fraught with great risks. How, for instance, could they prevent the rapidly expanding Home Forces from rising up too early and being annihilated by their vastly superior enemy in open battle? As their numbers grew, there was a growing and urgent desire among many resistance fighters to have a crack at the Germans after so many years of repression. How, too, could they prevent the Germans from launching a 'scorched earth' policy as they fled the country? There was also the danger of their own sabotage acts causing long-term damage to the Norwegian infrastructure and economy. Nor was there any guarantee that the Germans would leave the country at all, even if their forces collapsed on other fronts. There were widespread fears in Norway that Germany would try to hang on to some kind of Aryan empire in the north of Europe.

All plans from then on would have to be a careful balancing act between undermining the German war machine and not provoking a brutal crackdown or causing unnecessary damage to facilities vital to the Norwegians' welfare after the war. These challenges called for cool heads in Norway and in London, and for unity and discipline at all levels.

It was a testament to the restraint shown by Milorg and SOE that they were able to achieve all their objectives. In November 1943 Milorg and leaders of the civilian resistance issued a joint statement in which they declared that Norway should prepare itself but wait patiently for the reconquest of its country, making it clear that only catastrophe lay ahead if they rose up too soon. 'We are convinced that it will bring disasters to the people and the country which will be out of all proportion to the military gains, and that it will disrupt and destroy the longer-term work of civilian and military preparations which promise to be of the greatest importance to the nation,' the decree stated.

As the war swung the Allies' way and the Nazis reacted with ever greater barbarity towards the people, the patience of Milorg and the Norwegian populace was stretched to the limit. Executions and reprisals became more frequent, and in August 1943 1,100 police and former army officers were deported to

German concentration camps amid fears – justified to some extent – that many of their number were sympathetic to or working for the resistance. Being a member of both the Norwegian police and Milorg was a highly dangerous enterprise, and those who sought to undermine the Germans from within lived in constant fear of being exposed. Haugland, the W/T operator, recounts an incident in which three resistance fighters were driving into Oslo with a wireless set and some Sten and tommy guns in the back of their car. They were stopped by a German patrol, but as they were being led away three policemen arrived on the scene, all of them good Norwegians with contacts in the resistance. Insisting that the captured men were their responsibility, the Norwegian policemen bundled them into the back of their van and took them into town, saluting German patrols as they went, before releasing them and claiming later that they had, unfortunately, escaped from their custody.

When a fire broke out in Oslo University, Terboven saw his chance to punish the intellectuals he so despised by arresting hundreds of professors and students and sending them to camps. But attempts to mobilise workers for the German war economy as well as troops met with total failure. The German efforts to recruit Norwegian men for their campaign on the Eastern Front were farcically unsuccessful. Illustrated posters showing handsome, chiselled-jawed young Norwegians heading off to fight the Bolsheviks mocked the reality of the local reaction. Only a few thousand joined the 'crusade' against the Soviets. The small handful who had been there and survived generally refused to go back, many of them even throwing themselves out of first-storey windows to break their limbs.

Throughout the war, the occupiers' attempts to integrate

Norwegian people into their war machinery were met with stubborn refusal and contempt. Only a few thousand Norwegians had volunteered for labour in German factories, so in 1944 Terboven ordered all men born between 1921 and 1923 to present themselves at the Labour Office in Oslo. The Oslo detachment of SOE troops had discovered that all mobilisation cards had to pass through a processing machine before they were ready for issue, so they broke into the office and blew it up. Others simply did not turn up to register for the labour movement at the time appointed, and many of them fled to the mountains where they joined the resistance movement.

A final attempt to control the population by issuing new ration cards that would be withheld if men refused to cooperate with the Nazis was scuppered when Milorg received a tip-off and hijacked the train carrying the new cards. All German attempts to tame the Norwegians failed miserably.

The Norwegians waited with a mixture of hope, anxiety and patience following the D-Day landings on 6 June, 1944. When would their own day come? After a bridgehead had been established in France, General Eisenhower, the head of Allied forces in Europe, ordered that 30,000 more Norwegian resistance fighters should be recruited and trained in preparation for the final push against the Germans. But at the same time he issued a stern directive via the Norwegian High Command, warning that for its own sake the country must sit tight and do nothing until told otherwise. 'No Allied military offensives are planned for this theatre, therefore no steps must be taken to encourage the resistance movement to overt action, as no outside support can be forthcoming.' The heavy resistance of the Germans in France tied up the bulk of Allied forces, and a British division earmarked to assist in the liberation of Norway had instead to be sent across the Channel.

These were testing times for the men of the Norwegian resistance who had been trained to fight and who knew that Germany's defeat was now inevitable and that the liberation of other countries had already begun.

The main role of the resistance was to safeguard the most important installations of the country's infrastructure, such as power stations, dams, factories, transport and communication networks. (In Telemark there were fears that the Germans would blow the Møsvatn dam and wipe out not just the plant but the whole valley, killing the thousands of people living there.) The forces would emerge from their hideouts when given the signal to ensure that law and order were maintained. At the same time, they were to continue their limited sabotage and intelligence operations aimed at undermining the German military effort. In 1944, the Allies dropped 215 agents back into Norway to train the Home Forces for the final push to freedom, while camps housing up to 400 resistance recruits were established in the mountains.

Although the British were the nation that gave Norway the most support during the war, the first foreign troops to reach Norwegian soil were Russian as they pursued the retreating Germans through Finland and the Arctic. As the Germans withdrew, they torched the Finnmark region, wrecking the infrastructure and burning down towns and villages to slow the Russian advance. The policy led to widespread devastation as well as the displacement of 40,000 Norwegians, and served as a chilling cautionary tale for the Home Forces as they waited anxiously for the right moment to rise up.

Norwegians huddled around their radio sets as the Allies

slowly squeezed Germany to defeat on other fronts. On 7 May 1945, a week after Hitler's suicide, they listened to the announcement that his successor Dönitz had declared unconditional surrender on all fronts. The following day a British brigadier arrived in Oslo and contacted the German commanders, who agreed to an orderly retreat. As between forty and fifty thousand Milorg fighters emerged from the mountains to take temporary control of the country, wild celebrations were launched. Hundreds of thousands took to the streets and Norwegian flags waved wildly as the Germans prepared for a rapid evacuation. Many Nazis, Norwegian and German, including Terboven, committed suicide over the coming days, but there were remarkably few acts of aggression perpetrated by either side during the withdrawal. The following day, under the supervision of Milorg, a temporary civil administration was put in place, the concentration camps were opened and the arrest of collaborators began.

On 13 May, Crown Prince Olav, Norway's Supreme Commander, returned to Oslo with several members of the government-in-exile, and the celebrations reached a peak of joy when King Haakon VII set foot on home soil on 7 June. In December the King reopened the Storting, the parliamentary assembly.

No one knows exactly how many Norwegians were arrested or killed during those five terrible years. But according to official figures, 2,091 men and women of the resistance died either in action, by execution or inside concentration camps. In total, 40,000 Norwegians were interned in concentration camps, most of them at Grini, just outside Oslo. Of these 658 were killed or died in the camps. The fact that Norway had only a very small Jewish community partly explains the small number compared to the millions who died elsewhere across Europe. However, just as it was for the rest of occupied Europe, life under Nazi rule had been a traumatic and desperate experience for the Norwegians. But thanks to the Allies and the heroes of the SOE and Milorg, their country was returned to them.

ACKNOWLEDGEMENTS

There are dozens of people to whom I am indebted for their help in producing both the television documentary and this book, but I would like to single out a few for special thanks. The book would not have been written without Niall Edworthy's help. He spent many weeks at the Public Record Office and in Norway doing a brilliant research job and then drafting the text. His boundless enthusiasm and skill were the essential ingredients in creating the book under a very tight deadline. The BBC team have been great, particularly the producer/director Martin Pailthorpe, assistant producers Emma Jones and Danny Kane, cameraman Doug Allan and soundman Colin Bowes – all of them have been unstintingly generous with their time and help. Brian Desmond, our contact in Norway, was helpful beyond the call of duty. Without him, the documentary would simply not have been made. Rupert Lancaster at Hodder has been a thoughtful and energetic editor, calmly and steadily steering the project in the right direction, and I would also like to thank his assistant, Hugo Wilkinson. Our friends at the Norwegian end have also been tremendous, particularly Arfinn Moland and Ivar Kragland at Norway's Resistance Museum and Tor Nicolaysen, a connoisseur of our story and the owner of the charming

Rjukan Fjellstue hotel, a few kilometres from the Vemork hydro plant. Very special thanks, too, to the British and Norwegian soldiers who took part in the re-enactment of the story: the men of Harens Jegerkommando, particularly Tomas Adam Preben Ukvithe, and Royal Marine Mountain leaders Adam Rutherford and Jason Milne. Their professionalism was outstanding and together they proved that the spirit of 1942–1943 is still very much alive. The staff at the Public Records Office in Kew were also extremely helpful in helping me to comb through the vast stores of their archives for the relevant files. The files consulted were: HS/2/172, HS/2/173, HS/2/184, HS/2/185, HS/2/186, HS/2/187, HS/2/188, HS/2/189, HS/2/190.

The material for this book is based almost exclusively on thousands of original documents from the Public Record Office and BBC interviews with the survivors of the Gunnerside and Grouse operations themselves. For background research I have read a number of books about the Second World War in Europe, the Norwegian occupation and resistance and the Special Operations Executive. For further reading about SOE, I strongly recommend *The Secret History of SOE* by William MacKenzie, which was commissioned at the end of the war but not published until 2000, when all the documents on which it was based were finally declassified.

The author and the publishers would also like to thank Peter Fjagesund for his generosity and skill in correcting this text from a Norwegian point of view.

Special thanks also to Frode Saeland, a museum curator and local historian, who has spent many years studying the story and who has provided us with much valuable information.

PHOTOGRAPHIC
ACKNOWLEDGEMENTS

Photographs reproduced by permission of: Norges Hjemme-frontmuseum, Oslo: page 1, pages 4–5 (all); Ray Mears: page 6 (bottom), page 9, page 10 (bottom), page 11 (bottom), pages 12–13, page 14; National Archives, Kew: pages 2–3 (all), page 6 (top), page 7 (all), page 8, page 15; Martin Pailthorpe: page 10 (top), page 11 (top), page 16.

INDEX